Guidance For New Clinicians In A Chaotic World:

How To Practice Your Craft While Preserving Your Traditional Values

Guidance For New Clinicians In A Chaotic World:

How To Practice Your Craft While Preserving Your Traditional Values

Steven Melman, MA, LPC, LMFT

LIBERTY HILL PUBLISHING

Liberty Hill Publishing
555 Winderley Pl, Suite 225
Maitland, FL 32751
407.339.4217
www.libertyhillpublishing.com

Library of Congress Control Number: 2024914312

Paperback ISBN-13: 978-1-66289-946-1
Hard Cover ISBN-13: 978-1-66289-947-8
Ebook ISBN-13: 978-1-66289-948-5

Endorsements

"The mental health profession has been perverted into becoming an ideological remnant of what we were all once familiar with. Steve Melman's decades of experience as a clinician have motivated him to warn the public and other clinicians about the dire need to preserve common sense practices that have been proven successful and not to be swayed by boutique approaches that are rooted in far-left-wing religiosity. With his stories of real situations that he's faced in the field and his genuine care for every patient who's seeking help, Melman is sounding the alarm about how we've lost our way in hopes that it's not too late to steer us back on course for a healthier society."

Adam B. Coleman,
author of "Black Victim To Black Victor",
Op-Ed Writer, Public Speaker,
host of the "Breaking Bread" video series,
and the Founder of Wrong Speak Publishing.

"Steven Melman's book is a practical guide, long overdue, that empowers new clinicians to develop the confidence and competence they need at the start of their careers. It also provides valuable insights on how to maintain one's traditional values in the midst of today's transient trends.

Jack Jaffe, Ph.D., is the author of three books,
including "The New Psychologist at Cedar Crest Prison."

Table of Contents

Endorsements v
Introduction vii
Chapter 1: How I Came To Choose This Profession. 1
Chapter 2: Advice To The New Clinician. 7
Chapter 3: The Counseling & Education of Our Children and Adolescents 41
Chapter 4: Violence In The US & Sensible Solutions. 65
Chapter 5: Current & Perhaps Permanent Conditions Affecting The Mental Health In The U.S. 83
Chapter 6: The Counseling of Couples & Successful Techniques . . . 97
Chapter 7: Finding Success In Working With Affective Disorders, Substance Abuse & Schizophrenics 115
Chapter 8: Additional Topics That Need To Be Addressed 139
Chapter 9: So, You Really Want To Establish Your Own Private Practice. 167
Chapter 10: Additional Tips, Strategies & Final Thoughts 179

Introduction

THE FOLLOWING STORY may be personally relatable to the reader, or this reader may know a family member or friend with whom this story resonates. The year was 1968. An adolescent who was 13 was at the beginning of the 8th grade in Galveston, Texas. This individual enjoyed school from the 1st to the 7th grade, and he was with the peers he had grown up with. But, at the beginning of the 8th grade, two things happened: school seemed to have gotten harder than the previous year, and, for the first time, there were too many students to be put into the same 8th-grade class. So, this boy was separated from his friends and put into the other class where he virtually knew no one. He believed the school's administrators separated the classes based on students' grades. He felt like these school administrators had made a terrible mistake, and he would prove to them that he belonged in the class where his friends were. His mission became his obsession. He would stay up hours after his bedtime to complete homework assignments, and he truly believed he had to have straight A's to accomplish his goal of being reunited with his friends and prove he was just as bright.

His parents took him to a psychologist, where they were told that if they did not remove him from this environment, it might lead to "a nervous breakdown." He did not know what a nervous breakdown was, and even if he did, he would not have believed it could be a possibility. He was just intent on accomplishing his feat.

This boy's father told the family he had been offered a transfer to work in Dallas and accepted the position. Rather than this teenager to continue attending school in Galveston, he was sent to Dallas to live with relatives and attend school there. The move to Dallas was a temporary reprieve from the stress he had endured in Galveston. At the same time, when he moved to Dallas, his parents sold their home in Galveston and made preparations to join him in Dallas. His parents had taken him to more psychologists, where he was tested, and they were told that he had a "learning disability," specifically a "reading disability." These same psychologists made predictions to his parents by saying, "If your son graduates from high school, be proud of him because we do not believe he can make it in college." Even at his young age, he was not prepared to accept their predictions. He attended a private school for the next two years and did well there.

However, when he was being transferred back to a public high school, it was discovered that the private school was not accredited. Therefore, if this adolescent wanted to receive credit for the 8th and 9th grades, he would have to take a test in every subject he had taken in the private school to prove he belonged in the 10th grade. He recalled taking the academic examinations in the summer, and the building was not air-conditioned. He was anxiety-ridden that everything hinged on passing these tests. If he did not pass them, he feared he might have to repeat either the 8th grade or 9th grade or both.

When the results arrived, he realized he had passed every one of them! Then, he attended high school starting in the 10th grade and obtained his high school diploma there. It was a surprise to him when he learned that he had made the "honor roll" for the three years he was there.

Despite being told that he could never succeed in college, he was determined not only to be admitted but also to obtain his Bachelor's degree. In his adolescence, he decided he wanted to be a clinical psychologist. At the time, if one majored in psychology and wanted to be a therapist, one would have to obtain a Ph.D. By the time he had graduated from high school, his parents had moved to Tennessee. He applied to universities and colleges in that state. Even though his grades were more than acceptable, his entrance test scores were low.

As a result, only one university offered to admit him on a probationary basis, and he had to prove that he could pass his classes in order to remain at that university and earn his Bachelor's degree. However, he knew he could excel if he was given a chance. At the end of his first semester, he achieved a 3.0 average, which he maintained throughout his years at this university.

Along the way, his biggest challenge while attending this university was passing Statistics. It took him three times taking and dropping this class under three different instructors. At the end of the 3rd time dropping this class, he decided to do the two things he'd hoped would lead him to pass this course successfully. First, he asked the instructor if he could continue to sit in the class despite having dropped it, and he also befriended a classmate, Marty. Marty thought through situations "mathematically." Marty would use his mathematical skills when the average person expressed themselves using words. The boy learned a lot from Marty, and not just from statistics class. He learned how to play a card game called Cribbage, win free games in pinball, improve his tennis skills, and learn how to shoot pool. Due to Marty's mathematical sense, he was challenging to beat. For example, he could divide a pool table or tennis court into angles and play those angles. Marty knew combinations and permutations in Cribbage and played the odds, making him almost unbeatable. During a summer semester, this individual took the Statistics class for the fourth time with the same professor he had continued to sit in on his course after dropping it the previous semester. This time, he passed the class with a high B.

After graduating and obtaining his Bachelor's degree, he applied to graduate schools. He planned to acquire a Master's degree and then attain a Ph.D. Unfortunately, again, only one graduate school admitted him on a probationary basis. Déjà vu! He had been in this position before. He was only looking for one graduate school that would give him a chance, and he would do the rest to prove that he belonged in a graduate program. By the time he obtained his Master's degree in clinical psychology, he had achieved over a 3.0 average.

Although he still believed he would need a Ph.D. in psychology, he needed a break from school to recuperate. He was taking his time off from school when a job opened at the Wichita Falls Mental Health/Mental Retardation Center. They needed an intake counselor at the center and didn't need a Ph.D. He applied and was hired there. Eventually, the state of Texas offered Master's level counselors to take a test to be a Licensed Professional Therapist. He remembered talking to many individuals who would take the exam the next day, just as he was. Many were there to take the exam a second or third time because they couldn't pass it the first time. He took the exam and passed it the first time. Five years later, he obtained a Marriage and Family Therapist license. He concluded that he no longer needed a Ph.D. to achieve his goal of providing counseling. He believed he was now on his way to gaining the experience that would eventually lead him to attain his own private practice. However, as he began obtaining knowledge as a psychotherapist, he did not realize just how much graduate school had not prepared him to feel confident and competent. He recollected that it took him about two years to acquire those skills and the confidence to apply them.

There have been many colleagues who have taken him under their tutorage and mentored him. He will never forget those who helped him since he was about 13. He would like to thank the admissions departments at Memphis State University (where he obtained his Bachelor's degree) and Austin Peay State University (where he earned his Master's degree) for accepting him into their universities on a probationary basis. The years passed so quickly; the adolescent boy was now fully grown in all aspects of life, had achieved his goal of being a counselor, and had been in the mental health field for over 40 years.

His last employed position was that of a Federal EAP (Employee Assistance Program) as a Senior Consultant, and after 25 years, he retired in June 2021. In that role, he counseled federal employees and their family members and provided management consultations. He was an account manager to over 50 federal agencies and conducted presentations on about 50 different mental health topics. He also led critical incident stress management services to employees who were grieving the loss of a coworker or those seeking to cope with traumatic events such as a hurricane or tornado or the aftermath of the Oklahoma City bombing and the 9/11 terrorist attacks.

If you had told him he would be employed in a position where 60-75% of his time would be spent conducting presentations, he would not have believed it. For he recalled, as a youth, having extreme anxiety over having to speak in public. Over time, in his job with the Federal EAP, he overcame his fear of conducting presentations. There were instances when he presented to audiences as large as 500 attendees.

After he received his Master's degree and became licensed, his eventual career goal was to have a successful, full-time practice. However, after being employed with the Federal EAP both as a Consultant and then as a Senior Consultant, he came to appreciate the roles he provided. He loved the variety of his job responsibilities. While employed there, he decided to initiate a private practice but no longer intended to transition it to full-time. So, for the 25 years he was employed at the Federal EAP, he maintained a part-time private practice. Now, in retirement, he kept his private practice part-time.

He promised himself that he would seek to motivate others, whether they are clients or colleagues, especially children, and adolescents, as a counselor and as a mentor. Also, he would never make predictive statements as had been forecasted for him when he was an adolescent. Psychologists had attempted to predict his abilities from the results of psychological tests. He concluded that there is one thing that tests cannot measure, and that is one's motivation and desire. If an individual is committed to accomplishing their goals, there are a few things a person cannot achieve. He found that there had been many challenges he had faced, and it was the same for people he had encountered. He refused to allow people or circumstances to derail him from accomplishing his dreams and goals. He tried to instill that belief in others. We can refuse to accept the roadblocks that have been put in front of us. All we need to do is find the loophole(s) and the fortitude to meet those challenges. This belief and tenacity have served him well throughout his life.

Speaking of tenacity, he had many of that, like when he took a job at a residence hall in Oil City, PA, where the previous year, the students had damaged the dormitory to the sum of over $13,000. The year this individual was employed, the students vowed to double the damages to the residence hall. This individual could have coined the phrase, "Not on my watch!" One of the incidents that occurred that first semester was when a student, who was being removed from the dormitory, broke every window of this individual's vehicle with a baseball bat. The resident foolishly left the bat in the dormitory with his fingerprints on the bat. The student, with the help of a police detective, was prosecuted for the offense. The subject of this narrative was able to obtain the help of this detective to ensure no substantial damage to the residence hall occurred. They both patrolled the residence hall every night for the last month of that spring semester. It would have been easy for him to quit after his car's windows were broken, but he had committed himself to the entire academic year.

The last tidbit is just something interesting to relay. During his senior year at Memphis State University, he was hired part-time as a tour guide with Gray Line Tours. During his training in August of 1977, Elvis Presley died, and consequently, he was no longer being trained. That year, he gave tours of the city of Memphis and a separate tour of the life and memorabilia of Elvis' possessions.

You may be wondering who this person is whom I have been describing. I am that person, and everything I have related so far has been true and accurate. So again, perhaps, you can relate to my story. If not, maybe you know someone who has had similar experiences. The purpose of sharing my story was to convey that life is not fair, but if you want something, don't let anyone or anything stand in your way of accomplishing your goals.

For many years, I have had the urge to write this book. Initially, it was going to be written without addressing any social issues. All that changed when I took the class on Cultural Diversity. As I took that course, I wondered, then and now, why the author emphasized divisive concepts such as white privilege and white guilt when I believed the class should have emphasized how to be sensitive to different cultures. Then, as I continued to write this book, I was astounded by how rapidly our society and profession have changed, and we are being forced to accept and even embrace concepts that would not have been considered even ten years before this book was written. Some subjects I will discuss later in Chapter 8 include Cultural Diversity, Microaggressions, Critical Race Theory, Wokeism, Transgender Pronouns, Transgender Reaffirming Care, and Reassignment Surgeries.

So, why did I include this chapter? Because I believe someone in our field needed to push back against how liberal some leaders want to take our entire helping profession, which includes all counselors, psychologists, psychiatrists, teachers, and physicians. It is permissible to retain your values and principles. An organization was established to cater to us, and it is called the Association for Mental Health Professionals (AMPH).

I also hope that in writing this book, I can motivate others, whether they are newly degreed or newly licensed clinicians, whether they are children, adolescents, or adults. In addition, I hope to continue encouraging couples, whether married or living together, to achieve their mutual goals. Through my many years of providing counseling, I have been motivated to help clients, whether they were struggling with depression, bipolar, anxiety, substance abuse, or just life in general, to accomplish their therapeutic goals.

As stated previously, I was knowledgeable about clinical theories when I achieved my Master's degree. Still, I certainly did not feel confident or fully competent in successfully helping clients accomplish their goals. I hope that by the time the reader has finished this book, they will have acquired that confidence and competence.

I further hope this book is beneficial to graduate students, those newly licensed and those who are new to the profession. In subsequent chapters, I included many clinical examples. I want these examples and this book to help you grow as a professional and put you on a path to becoming more competent and confident in achieving these aspirations more quickly. So please take this journey with me, as I hope you will find this book practical, relatable, entertaining, informative, and inspiring.

CHAPTER 1:

How I Came To Choose This Profession

AT AN EARLY age, I have always been introspective. I wanted to make a difference in my little corner of the world. I wanted my life and career to be rewarding and meaningful and to help my fellow man. As I explored the meaning of my life, I not only wanted to help others find theirs but also to help inspire and motivate others to do and be the best they can be. I was not looking to be famous or remembered by future generations, but I did want to know that I had assisted others throughout my career and life. That list would extend not only to clients but also to colleagues, friends, and family members.

As I explored the field of psychology and as a psychotherapist, I found it to be a match to what I was searching for belongingness to a profession, love for humanity, the need for importance, and respect. My parents were friends with a clinical psychologist and his wife, and a couple of times a year, I met with him and conducted informational interviews. During those meetings, I asked him every question imaginable about the profession, the tasks of a psychologist, and what advice he could offer me as I considered this profession and a potential career. Nothing he said was a discouragement. After those meetings with this psychologist, I decided at the time to be just like him and eventually have a full-time private practice just as quickly as I could achieve that goal.

When you are young, time seems to move at a snail's pace. In junior high and high school, there weren't any psychology or counseling classes that were offered, but my enthusiasm remained stoked!

Psychology 101 was the first class I enrolled in as a freshman at what was then Memphis State University; it is now referred to as the University of Memphis.

I still remember that first day of class. The course was held in a large auditorium-type classroom. The two instructors came in and sat on the desk on the stage. They spoke of their love for psychology and how they would teach the course and the textbook, each teaching various chapters. I remember it like it was yesterday. I looked around the auditorium and said to myself, "Yep, this is the profession and career for me. I now know this is where I am supposed to be."

I began my career in the mental health field in 1983. I cannot express my gratitude to the psychologist and supervisor who hired me as an Intake Counselor at the Wichita Falls Mental Health Mental Retardation Center, also referred to as the Wichita Falls MHMR Center. Looking back to the beginning of my career, I could not have asked for a better entry-level position where I first gained experience conducting intakes and comprehensive assessments.

In performing those assessments, I also was able to master the Diagnostic Statistical Manual (DSM). Every Friday, the other intake specialists and I would bring our intakes to a staff meeting and would present them. Then, the outpatient clinicians would agree to take our intakes and provide counseling. On one particular Friday, I arranged my intakes from the routine to the more interesting ones. And then, I saved the best one for last and referred to it as "the case of the week," and that became my routine. During the week, the staff would ask if I had a "case of the week yet." Sometimes, I would defy the odds by presenting multiple cases of the week!

Eventually, at the MHMR, I became a therapist, still conducting intakes, but now I was also providing counseling to virtually every client assigned to me. Also, there was a psychiatrist on staff who sometimes would allow me to sit in on his psychiatric evaluations with our shared patients. From him, I learned about psychotropic medications, and I was able to ask his rationale for prescribing one medication over another. To this day, I still try to keep up with the prescribed drugs, recommended dosages, potential side effects, etc.

Again, as previously noted, another job responsibility at the MHMR was working with the Wichita County mental health judge when patients had been involuntarily admitted to the Wichita Falls Mental Hospital. My role was to interview those patients at the hospital, look at the patient's hospital records, interview the hospital staff, and then write a report to the judge offering my clinical judgment. My evaluation would help the judge determine whether the patient needed to continue being committed to the hospital or if the patient could be discharged and services could be provided on an outpatient basis. However, after three years, I was ready for new experiences, continued to learn new skills, honed those I had already acquired, and went on to Big D (Dallas).

So, what were my job responsibilities as a Caseworker III? I provided the following services while employed at the Wichita Falls MHMR from 1983 to 1986:

- Provided assessments and counseling to individuals, couples, and families.
- Screened individuals for referral to the Wichita Falls State Hospital.
- Interviewed family members who believed their loved one needed to be involuntarily committed to the Wichita Falls State Hospital.
- Conferred with the county mental health judge to determine the appropriate treatment for court-committed individuals.

After resigning from the Wichita Falls MHMR, I moved to Dallas, where I continued my career. The following two positions were at the

Family Guidance Center for five years and then at Personal Performance Consultants for another five years. I had further opportunities to hone my clinical counseling skills at each of these counseling locations. And lastly, I spent the last 16 of the 25 years of my employment career as a Federal Employee Assistance Program (EAP) Consultant. I worked with federal agencies, their supervisors, and employees throughout my employment there. As stated earlier, I gained additional experience providing counseling and acquiring skills in conducting supervisor consultations, presentations, and CISDs (Critical Incident Stress Debriefings). I was promoted to an EAP Senior Consultant in the last seven years. I never wanted to vie for the supervisor position, but I did enjoy mentoring fellow EAP consultants in my Senior Consultant position. When I decided to retire from this position and from the employment world, I believed I had achieved all the goals I had sought.

Below is a list of duties I provided while employed at the Federal EAP 1996-May 2021:

- Assessment and brief EAP counseling to federal employees and their family members.
- Provide account management to federal agencies and their supervisors.
- Conduct presentations on a variety of mental health topics.
- Conduct Critical Incidence Debriefing and Grief Groups to federal employees.
- Mentored newly hired and seasoned consultants to help them acquire the needed skills to succeed.

At about the same time, I began employment with the Federal EAP, and I believed I was finally ready to establish a private practice with the intent of transitioning from part-time to full-time. However, I came to appreciate having the best of both worlds. I could continue my private practice part-time while having full-time benefits from the Federal EAP and acquiring additional skills. I also learned something about myself. As much as I love counseling, I needed variety, and my full-time job provided just that. In my employment with the Federal EAP, I did not see an abundance of counseling clients, maybe 1 or 2 a day. The rest of my day was spent gaining experience in those other areas: conducting management consultations, presentations, etc. So, I certainly did not feel burned out seeing an additional 2 to 3 clients each evening in my private practice. When I started my private practice many years ago, I knew I would want to continue my private practice part-time when I retired. Even though I am not sure I had ever scripted my career, it seemed to have fallen into place as though it had been well planned out all along.

I have met colleagues throughout my various jobs and careers, whether they were Master's level, Ph. D.s, or psychiatrists. I believe it is essential to network with other colleagues. Therefore, I would refer clients as appropriate and warranted once my network was established with professional contacts who shared our mutual treatment philosophies.

Now, in retirement, I continue seeing clients in my private practice part-time while agreeing to conduct presentations on various mental health topics and provide CISDs with client companies. Yet, after all these years, I ended as I began, with a love and passion for the field of psychology, helping clients, couples, and families accomplish their counseling goals.

I recently discovered a term paper I had written before I entered my career; I composed the following words: "So when it came to choosing a career, I wanted one that would also define the life I wanted to lead. Long after I retire, I want to be able to look back upon my career as being rewarding, meaningful, and offering something to my fellow man." I believe I accomplished the goals I set for myself

40 years later. No one knows what life has in store for us. But as long as I am able, both physically and mentally, I want to continue my private practice and continue my involvement in psychology. I want to help clients achieve their goals and assist colleagues in their quest to become more confident and competent as they pursue their career in this gratifying field.

CHAPTER 2:

Guidance For New Clinicians In A Chaotic World

Advice To The New Clinician

ULTIMATELY, IT DOESN'T matter very much what theory a therapist subscribes to; what matters more is the rapport that a clinician has established with their client(s). After many years of research and replication, this still remains true. What is important to me in building rapport with clients is bringing my competence and authenticity, personality, sense of humor, and even personal stories to help clients know and understand that we are all struggling with similar issues and challenges. In addition, I want to teach clients skills they can employ in counseling as well as in their lives. The last thing I want for my clients is to become dependent upon therapy. There's an old saying that is usually attributed to Anne Isabella Thackeray Ritchie, a British writer. It appears that she was the first to use this expression in the late 1800s, which she did in her book, "Mrs. Dymond." Ms. Ritchie's quote is: "Give a man a fish, and you feed him for a day. Teach a man to fish, and you've fed him for a lifetime." I look upon therapy like that. My job with my clients is to work myself out of a job. I teach clients and couples how to problem solve and use/implement those skills to solve current and future challenges.

It is vital that we, as clinicians, need to examine our values and ethics as we provide therapy to our clients. For example, I just mentioned that my job as a therapist with my clients is to work myself out of a job. And yet, I know some colleagues have helped their clients achieve their goals, only to have the therapist invent more therapeutic goals to keep the client in counseling. In my private practice, I am confident that I have never kept clients in therapy because I needed to make up for my expenses. I am about to say something you may find hard to believe. When the number of clients falls below my desired number, I will say, "I sure could handle a new or return client in my practice." I don't know who or how my prayers are being answered, but mysteriously, I begin receiving calls from potential clients. All I can say is try it and see if it works for you. You have nothing to lose.

The therapist a client chooses should make them feel comfortable, and the client should see their psychotherapist as being competent and personable in helping them set and accomplish their goals. The client ought to ask themselves how well this therapist relates to and understands their issues and allows them to problem-solve their way through their challenges by teaching them skills they can apply while in therapy and throughout the rest of their lives. As a therapist, I like to paint mental pictures for my clients. I sometimes use this one that women may relate to in the following analogy. There are many bedazzling shoes that say, "Buy me," but when you try them on and walk around, they don't feel comfortable. Choosing a counselor is very similar. There are a lot of therapists to choose from, even some recommended by friends and family members. In the end, clients should choose the one they feel comfortable with, relate to, and whom they think can help them accomplish their counseling goals.

As stated in the previous chapter, I believed I needed a Ph.D. in clinical psychology to be able to provide therapy. I had every intention of obtaining my Ph.D. eventually. However, I was hired at the Wichita Falls MHMR Center without having a Ph.D. Then, in Texas, in the 1980s, the Licensed Professional Counselor and the Licensed Marriage and Family Therapist came along. It suddenly became apparent to me that one could practice counseling without having a Ph.D. once they had acquired these licenses. In a four-year Ph.D. program, one spends two years learning clinical skills and an additional two years learning how to become a researcher and is encouraged to publish articles. Although I see the importance of research, reading, and understanding studies, for me, providing counseling and helping clients accomplish their goals was the direction I wanted to take in my career.

The following was the first piece of advice given to me by a colleague as I began pursuing my career at my first job. When I was hired for my first counseling position at the MHMR Center, I had a client I had seen for several sessions. We had accomplished some of her goals, and this client decided to take a break from counseling. When she decided to resume, she saw a colleague of mine. In one of her sessions, she confided in my colleague that although I was quite helpful and caring, I was perhaps too serious and stiff as a counselor. My colleague and friend took me aside and gave me some great advice: "You have a great personality and a great sense of humor. You will be a better and more successful therapist when you bring those traits into the sessions with your clients." It took a while for me to accept his advice. I believed I had to take a client's problems very seriously, and offering humor in session might be interpreted as demeaning and insincere. In time, I was able to follow his suggestions, and he was right. Now, it is part of what I say to clients in the first session. "I take very seriously what brings you to counseling. I believe it is possible for us to achieve your counseling goals and, at the same time, have fun. I also want you to recommend me to others, telling them that counseling can help them resolve their issues and, at the same time, therapy can also be enjoyable, not something dreaded." I have included my use of bringing my sense of humor into counseling in my biography write-up with Psychology Today. And clients have given me feedback that it was part of why they chose me when making their first appointment.

Again, I can't emphasize enough to bring your personality and sense of humor into your sessions. As an adolescent, I found a way of adding levity to the classroom without completely disrupting what a teacher wanted to teach each day. I know the example I will share with you is pretty silly. When I was in junior high school, teachers would enter the classroom every day, and they would ask me to "turn around" because I was talking with a classmate behind me. Then, one day, it struck me to comply differently. When one particular teacher asked me to "turn around," I stood up, turned a full 360 degrees, and sat back down in the same position I was initially in, ready to talk again with the classmate behind me. I then turned to face the teacher and complied with his request. I wanted the teacher to know that I was implicitly following his instructions. I use the technique of having fun in counseling. When a client or a married couple has put forth a lot of effort in a session, I will take the opportunity to take a break to find something we can laugh about. It might be a joke or the way something was phrased during the session. Finding humor in a session relaxes the couple or client and puts them at ease while building rapport. It also allows the client or couple and therapist to return to the issue at hand as they continue to resolve it. In an attempt to offer an example of a joke, I might tell a client or couple. "What do you get when you play a country-western song backward? You get your spouse back, your dog back, your job back, etc."

Along with having fun in sessions, I also tell my clients and couples that I want to be one of the most optimistic therapists that they could have in their corner. For example, if I see a married couple for counseling, I would never tell them that the best thing they could do is divorce. Quite the contrary, it is my role as a vehicle to help them achieve their marital goals. To do otherwise would remind me too much of the psychologists who told my parents what I could and couldn't accomplish. It is the couple's decision to stay together or not. My role is not to predict their ability to stay married and find happiness.

There are many theories and psychotherapies in which one can put one's faith. Over the years, I became an eclectic therapist, choosing from several techniques as each situation warrants. However, I often use Cognitive Behavioral Therapy (CBT) and Motivational Interviewing (MI). I believe CBT is the most commonsensical, logically based technique for the therapist and the easiest for clients to follow.

Cognitive-Behavioral Therapy (CBT) is a directive therapy. The therapist leads the process, teaching patients how to develop effective coping methods for various problems, including depression, anxiety, panic disorders, and many more. The therapy sessions are structured and focused. Cognitive-behavioral therapy is based on the idea that the person has difficulties because of faulty or irrational thinking and behaviors. Often, these clients' distorted thinking resorts to self-criticism, guilt, or excessive criticism of others.

During sessions, clients learn coping techniques by learning practical, more productive ways to respond to distressing or anxiety-provoking situations or feelings. For example, a cognitive-behavioral therapist examines a client's thoughts and beliefs. One's thoughts and beliefs can be rational or irrational. First, this therapist would diplomatically challenge those thoughts and beliefs that are irrational. Then, collaboratively, the therapist and client would discuss how the client can change those beliefs and thoughts to become more rational. The therapist also suggests behaviors that reinforce and solidify more rational thoughts and beliefs. Finally, using the CBT model, the therapist assigns homework to the client and asks them to keep track of thoughts, feelings, and situations. The results of the client's assignment will be discussed in the next therapy session. In future chapters, examples will be offered to show how cognitive-behavioral techniques can be utilized in working with clients and their presenting issues.

I often use Motivational Interviewing when clients are challenged with a choice they need to make or when they are struggling with substance use or abuse. Motivational Interviewing (MI) "is a collaborative, goal-oriented style of communication with particular attention to the language of change. It is designed to strengthen personal motivation for and commitment to a specific goal by eliciting and exploring the person's own reasons for change within an atmosphere of acceptance and compassion." (Miller & Rollnick, 2013, p. 29). In a later chapter, I will expand on examples of how I use MI.

Many years ago, I was offered the opportunity to take over a colleague's private practice in a rural area, east of Dallas. This colleague gave me a very nice compliment. When he thought of whom he wanted to offer his practice to, he thought of me first, even though I had a day job and a separate private practice in Dallas. He said I had a particular way of conversing with clients, whether they lived in Dallas or a rural area. He said that rather than trying to impress clients with my education and vocabulary, I could relate to clients in a down-to-earth way without using psychological jargon or terms that clients may not understand. Relating to clients using everyday language helps them see their clinician as being on the same level as them. Also, it allows clients to see their clinician as being non-judgmental. Yes, I have some insights, experiences, and education. Still, I don't have to impress them with my education or use complicated terms. Hopefully, being down to earth with them will lead them to trust me and believe I have their best interests in mind. I achieved this by how I wanted to connect and relate with them.

I remember when I began seeing clients early on in my career. I was so focused on myself and what my replies should be. I became a more effective therapist when I started having conversations with clients, asking questions for more clarification, and sometimes just listening. This took the pressure off me, always having to come up with brilliant, insightful solutions to clients' issues. When I learned to have conversations with a client or a couple, I would often come up with a response or offer something that might be insightful from the flow of the conversation. Sometimes, during a session, the client would recall something significant that I had said that resonated with them. Then, there would often be that "aha" moment where they say, "Well, that makes sense."

As a Federal EAP counselor/consultant, I conducted presentations on various mental health topics. My fear of public speaking went back to grade school, and now I spend about 60-75% of my day job conducting training in that position. The advice is the same in this category as it is in being an effective therapist. Take the focus off of yourself, off of your emotions and fears, and emphasize the topic you are presenting.

Often, your audiences are not experts. They are waiting to hear the results of the presenter having prepared the material, rehearsing, and finding a way of connecting with the audience. I connected with audiences through humor, authenticity, responsiveness, and listening to their questions and comments.

I believe that I can work with virtually any client, no matter their culture, race, or religion. Sometimes, in therapy, especially in marital counseling, I will ask the individual or the couple to educate me on their culture or religion if those things are important to them. This allows me to be even more effective in the way I respond and connect with them based on what is significant to them. This is an example of collaboration between the client/couple and the therapist. The therapist helps them resolve the issue(s) that brought them to therapy while the clients are educating the counselor on those things that are important to them: again, their culture, religion, etc. I will share my thoughts about cultural diversity later on in Chapter 6.

Early on in my counseling career, I was working with a supervisor who, in my mind, was very assertive. I believed at the time that I wanted to emulate her skill of being assertive with my clients as she was with hers. There was a thin wall separating her office from mine, and some of the things she would say to her clients would make my jaw drop open. I couldn't believe that her clients did not bolt from her office. Looking back, she wasn't assertive; she was aggressive, but she could get away with it because it was part of her personality. Her clients saw her as having their best interests in mind. If I had tried to imitate her, my clients would probably have seen me as trying to be someone I wasn't because it just was not part of my personality.

Several years later, I was in group supervision with colleagues. A coworker brought up one of her client's cases and said she was stuck. Her client had begun therapy with her, stating that he wanted to work on one issue, but in completing the intake, she believed this client was abusing alcohol. She wasn't confident in addressing his alcohol abuse since he had not acknowledged that it was a problem for him. When it was my turn to offer advice to this colleague, I suggested that she go ahead and work with him and help him achieve his goal with the issue that brought him to counseling. If she had successfully helped him resolve that problem, she would have established some credibility with her client. She would then be free to ask if they could go back to the information he provided during the intake regarding his pattern of alcohol consumption. Hopefully, the client would see her as having his best interests at heart when discussing his alcohol abuse after they resolved the issue that brought him to therapy. After this group supervision session ended, this coworker came to my office and said the next time she was "stuck with a client," she would come to me for advice first. When I asked why she thought I was "diplomatically assertive," she said I could address issues with clients in a way that does not put them on the defensive. She said my approach allows clients to be receptive to consider issues they had not included in their original goals.

Earlier in my life, personally and professionally, I struggled to be more assertive. Over time, I have concluded that assertiveness is on a continuum, with passivity on one end and aggressive on the other, and assertiveness is somewhere in the middle. It is also possible for every individual to find a way to fit assertiveness into their personality in a way that makes them feel comfortable. To accomplish any goal, including wanting to become more assertive, for some, that may mean they learn to be less passive, while others want to be less aggressive. We, as humans, do not make quantum leaps in changes. Instead, the progress made towards any goal is incremental, "baby steps." Let me paint this mental picture to illustrate this. Imagine if an individual is taking a trip across the US by car. Suppose that person focuses on how many miles they have to travel and how long it will take them to accomplish that goal. In that case, they may become emotionally pessimistic and perhaps depressed. On the other hand, the individual may focus on shorter distances to achieve each hour and each day. They could distract themselves from the scenery around them and maybe listen to their favorite songs along the way. So, from this illustration, the individual emphasizes the journey, and if they don't give up, they will arrive at their destination. This is true for setting and accomplishing every goal we want to achieve in life. In my opinion, setting and achieving goals is what makes life worth living. Once we achieve one goal, relish in our accomplishment and then set the next destination (goal).

I want to offer my advice to clinicians who are considering going into private practice. I believe one should postpone going into private practice until they have had sufficient supervision. In my case, I started a part-time private practice after being employed in various clinical settings. It took me about ten years of gaining the necessary experience before I believed I was ready to initiate a private practice. I certainly am not advocating that everyone wait as long as I did. Suppose a clinician is considering joining managed care and insurance companies. In that case, most will not allow counselors to be on their provider panels until they have been providing therapy for at least two years after being licensed. Consider, if you will, that many clinicians do not receive supervision after opening a private practice office. So, again, I suggest postponing opening a private practice office and working at a counseling center, whether for-profit or non-profit, to hone the therapist's skills while also helping the counselor gain confidence and competence. I believe it has made me a better therapist by waiting. Indeed, it has made me a well-rounded clinician. I would also like to recommend that one consider continuing to receive supervision even after establishing their private practice. I will have more to say about establishing a private practice in Chapter 9.

When I decided to open a private practice office, I decided to be on managed care and insurance provider panels since most individuals seeking counseling have EAP and/or insurance benefits. Yet, when I applied to be on those panels as a therapist practicing in Dallas, I was told that Dallas was so saturated with counselors that no more clinicians were being added to their panels. I believed this was very discriminatory at the time and that they had opened themselves up to be sued. However, I thought that even I sued them, how long would it take for the suit to come to court, that is, if a judge would allow it?

Remember earlier, I related that a good part of my life often had been comprised of many loopholes. So, when others told me what I wanted was not achievable and yet very important to me, I always accepted that as a challenge. Often, others have established the loopholes or workarounds before us and all we have to do is follow in their "footsteps."

Coincidently, I had become friends with a clinician who had a successful private practice in Commerce, Texas. I had once told him how envious I was of him. About a year or two later, he approached me and asked if I wanted to take over his practice as he had decided to close his practice. When he informed me of the number of panels he was on (many were the same ones I had sought and were denied), I contacted them and told them I was considering taking over my colleague's practice. They informed me that they needed me in Commerce and the surrounding area and said I could also be on their panels in Dallas. That convinced me to take over his practice. I kept my practice in Dallas while also practicing in Commerce for nine years. I enjoyed practicing in Commerce and enjoyed the clients there, but after nine years, the hour-and-a-half drive each way eventually got the best of me. When I found someone to take over the practice in Commerce, I was able to remain on all the panels serving clients in the Dallas area. So, do not accept what is told to us as the gospel. Again, if something is important to you, find the workaround, find the loophole, and prove them wrong, even if we never have the opportunity to say it to them personally. It has always been gratifying that I could say in my head that what they told me was not achievable; I achieved them all and more. I proved them wrong!

This is but one example. My life has been filled with these challenges, and I have had to find the loopholes to these barriers that were put in front of me. Yet, that tenacity, persistence, and never-give-up attitude has always been inside me, and I try to pass along these characteristics to clients.

I ascribe and encourage clients to have and keep a positive attitude, acknowledge the goals they want to achieve, and state them out loud, even publicly. Sometimes, when you want something, opportunities present themselves. Sometimes, all you have to do is be aware of those opportunities and then go after them. Put your faith in your abilities, and then don't allow anyone or anything to prevent you from accomplishing your goals.

I want to show the following Iceberg Illusion that encapsulates my view of what others see when you, the therapist, have been successful in obtaining your goal of receiving your degree and licensure. That is visible above the surface. However, below the surface are the attributes you employed to accomplish your goals that are not seen by others. Those traits include hard work, dedication, sacrifices, disappointments, setbacks, persistence, never giving up, and never waving a white flag.

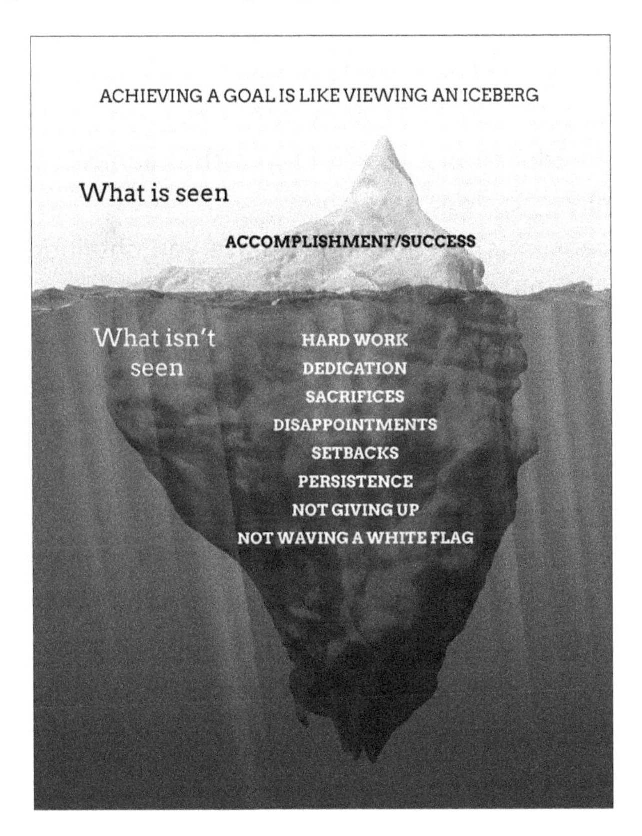

You will notice words like "failure" were not used because I want to convey encouragement. You can acknowledge that there will always be challenges in life, and seeing them as such motivates us as opposed to seeing them as obstacles. Often, we tend to avoid obstacles. But the perception of seeing them as challenges stokes us and motivates us to meet them and overcome them.

When I first began to consider that graduate school had not adequately provided me with that feeling of competence and confidence, I wanted to confirm those beliefs with my colleagues. I devised a questionnaire for those colleagues and asked them to complete it. Here is a copy of the questionnaire and a summary of their responses:

Interview Questionnaire For Clinicians

1. What degree did you obtain? Responses were a Ph.D., MA in Counseling and Guidance, MSSW, Masters in Ed, MA/MS in Clinical Psychology, Masters in Divinity, MA in Counseling Psychology & an MA in Educational Psychology with emphasis on Marriage and Family.
2. What licensure(s)/certification(s) have you obtained? Licenses: Licensed Clinical MH Counselor, LPC, LMFT, LICSW, PsyD, Substance Abuse Professional, Clinical Forensic Counselor. Certifications include CEAP (Certified Employee Assistance Professional), Crisis Response Specialist, Certified Anxiety Treatment Specialist & an LMFT in California.
3. How many total years have you been a clinician? The years of experience from those surveyed ranged from 14 to over 42 years.
4. What, if any, professional organizations are you a member of ? NASW, EAPA, APA, California AMFT, National Cognitive Behavioral Association, American Institute of Stress, The American Christian Counselors Association, and The International Critical Incident Stress Foundation.

5. What is your theoretical orientation? Do you share this with your clients? Theoretical Orientations ranged from CBT, Positive Psychology, Faith Perspective, Systems approach, Psychodynamic, Solution Focused Brief Therapy, Client-Centered and Eclectic from many years of practice; CBT with Motivational Interviewing. Some of the respondents said they don't share this info with their clients, while others said sharing this info is one of the reasons clients seek out these clinicians.
6. Are you employed, and if so, are you employed full-time or part-time? All of the respondents who did not have a private practice were all full-time employees.
7. If you have a private practice, is it a full-time or part-time practice? For those who were employed full-time in their day job and had a private practice, it was a part-time practice. For those who have a private practice, some of their practices were full-time. At the same time, some did other things in addition to providing therapy, and some intentionally kept their practices part-time (some of these clinicians are of age to collect social security).
8. When you first obtained your degree and/or became licensed, did you feel confident/competent to help your clients accomplish their goals? Approximately how long did it take you to achieve that confidence/competence if you didn't? Was there anything you did to help you feel that confidence and competence? With this last question, feel free to fully elaborate. Some of the respondents said they did feel competent and confident upon obtaining their degree and licensure. For those who didn't, here are some of their statements: "It took me a couple of years to feel confident. Luckily, I had excellent clinical supervision, which is critical in the early years." "I felt far from confident and did not feel school had prepared me for the work world. My confidence grew with experience and mentorship. In Massachusetts, you need two years of mentorship before one can be fully licensed." "Not entirely it took 3-5 years of experience, trial, and error to feel competent." "At first,

not at all." "I felt reasonably confident in helping clients achieve their goals, as I worked for 10 years in a paraprofessional capacity. Experience does come with time and patience, and talking with colleagues helped me feel confident. I also sought professional consultation to help me with my issues if I felt they may get in the way with a client."

9. What advice would you offer to newly licensed clinicians? "Be patient, open-minded, open ears, don't be so hard on yourself, and each day is a learning process." "There are many ways to practice your clinical skills." "Continued education helped a lot. Keeping up with evidenced-based treatments and consultation with other experienced clinicians." "Don't impose your own goals and values on your clients; listen to them; they are the experts on themselves." "Join a consultation group." "Find a mentor whose style is compatible with yours. Taking a lot of CEUs helped. Consider entering into therapy yourself to become your best self." "Read, Read, Read." "Hang out with seasoned clinicians and psychiatrists to call on as needed." "Be patient. Meet your clients where they are. Don't over-diagnose clinically. Stay curious! Get professional help if needed for yourself or with a case when you can't connect with a client. Don't be afraid to refer a client to another colleague, you can't help everyone! Enjoy working with a variety of people and learn from your clients!

The following questions are for folks who have established and are maintaining a private practice:

1. What type of practice do you have? Do you do other things besides providing counseling, such as conducting presentations, conducting CISMs, etc.? "My practice consists of referrals mainly from EAPs." "I have a coaching business, and I do public speaking engagements." "I see clients for various issues, and I also conduct presentations and conduct psychoeducational evaluations." "I do

corporate trainings, and I have contracts with companies and federal agencies providing services to supervisors and employees." "I have a small practice of long-term clients, EAP clients, and insurance clients. I work with ages 14 and up-individuals, couples, and families. Being retired, I am only doing counseling."

2. If you were to start over in your private practice, is there anything you would do differently, given what you have learned through experience? "Set my fees and don't apologize for them, and I would limit my practice to no more than 40% insurance dependent." "In my coaching business, I do not take insurance because it's not therapy; it's coaching, and also, it frees me up from being limited by the insurance company's regulations." "Not really. Initially, I sought to join insurance panels, but at the time, the panels only accepted new counselors with specific specialties. Therefore, I concentrated on EAP clients and am glad that I never got involved with insurance panels after hearing colleagues complain about the headaches caused by dealing with insurance companies." "No, I was fortunate and had some jobs that allowed me to learn the counseling ropes and counted towards my licensed hours."
3. From the time you became licensed, did you immediately start your practice, or were you employed elsewhere first, and if so, how long did you wait before starting your own practice? "I was employed elsewhere and did not start a private practice until 13 years later when I became unemployed." "I have been a full-time employee my entire career. I started my coaching business in 2013." "Was always employed elsewhere. My private practice has always been part-time." "I graduated in 2006 and began my private practice in 2007." "I worked in a community health center and was a program director at a hospital. I managed a practice with 3 other clinicians for a few years and then went into private practice." "I did start my practice immediately after getting my license as an LMFT. I started assertiveness training groups and women's self-care groups to get clients."

4. How long did it take for you to establish your practice? "8 months." "Started right away." "A couple of years since I did my coaching business part-time." "I don't recall, but I think it was a matter of months before I saw my first private client." "2-3 years."
5. Do you have a specialty? "Grief and loss, although as an EAP counselor, it has been important to be able to competently counsel clients with a wide variety of presenting issues." "I am a Money Empowerment Coach." "Family, adolescent and couples therapy. Brief strategic therapy along with long-term psychodynamic therapy." "Clinical Psychology" "I work with couples and clients dealing with anxiety, and I provide work-life coaching." "Not really. I am known to be fair and flexible within the gay community and diversity of races and ethnic groups in an EAP company and insurance companies I contract with."
6. Are you using any marketing techniques that you have found helpful that you would like to share? "I blog, I do podcasts, am visible on social media, and am connected to a lot of colleagues who refer to me." "I market through networking groups and word of mouth." "I still believe starting self-help groups (time-limited weeks) helps build a practice. Once someone chooses insurance companies, the referrals come through more easily. Volunteering while working on getting licensed hours in community-based organizations can help. Having a sliding fee scale can also help."
7. What do you experience as the pros and cons of a private practice? Pros: "Freedom to establish my own schedule and documentation methods, and I choose the clients I want to help." "It's mostly pros since I do it part-time, and I am not dependent on it for income. I do it because it's creative, and my coaching business is a different way of serving others." "Flexible hours with scheduling around my or my family's needs helped. Set my own fee and decorate the office the way I want. Cons: "Consultation is not as readily available." "Having your own practice can be expensive, clients

not considering your time and absenteeism; you are on your own and fear being sued." "Can be isolating and lonely at times."

8. Is your practice solo, or are you part of a group practice? If you have been in both, what are the pros and cons of each? "I have a partner, so we divide up the expenses." "I am solo, and it works for me because I control my own schedule." "I am a solo practice at this time. For many years, I shared office space with colleagues, and we each had our own office but shared a waiting room. It was helpful to have other therapists around."
9. Do you contract with managed care and/or insurance companies? If so, what percentage of your clients come from managed care? With insurance? "90% from insurance and just a few from other EAPs I worked with." One respondent broke her practice into the following: "30% managed care/insurance companies, 50% EAP companies, and 20% private pay." Some of the respondents said they do not work with insurance companies or managed care.
10. Do you have suggestions for setting up an office? "Subletting from another clinician is ideal when starting out or with a small practice." "I do all my coaching by phone or through Zoom." "Keep it simple. Consider using a billing service." "Seek consultation from others who have had an office for a while; consider getting on insurance panels and/or joining EAPs at least initially; set reasonable fees, promote through social media, and be patient." "Make the office a calm setting and private."
11. What suggestions can you offer to avoid professional burnout? "Consultation groups and maintaining a work-life balance." "Self-care. Take time off from time to time, breathe, have hobbies, and connect with colleagues." "Read for pleasure, something completely unrelated to the field." "Personal empowerment leads to professional empowerment. When you work on your self-worth, boundaries, and communicating your needs, then your professional work will support you as well." "Networking with other colleagues; appropriate spacing of appointments to give yourself

adequate time to decompress and complete your progress notes."
"Take care of yourself first-it gets scary in the beginning. Recognizing that you cannot help everyone and some clients are no-shows or stop counseling altogether, and you won't know why. Take time to do enjoyable activities, exercise, meditate, hobbies, get rest, and keep a sense of wonder and humor."

12. How many clients do you typically see weekly in your practice? "In part-time practices, the figures ranged from 4-11. In full-time practices, the figure was between 11-15, but seeing clients was augmented by other things such as conducting presentations, networking, etc."
13. Do you have any advice you would like to share on protecting yourself from lawsuits, complicated legal issues with clients, and potential complaints to the Start Board? "Don't over-diagnose, stay within your boundaries, and get supervision and consultation often." "Seek assistance from colleagues and an attorney with troubling clients; keeping abreast of malpractice issues and avoiding dual relationships." "Never practice without malpractice insurance." "Take an ethics course once a year." "Layout your terms and policies ahead in a confidentiality statement with the client at the beginning of the first session (most state professional organizations have samples to review). Check in with your clients regularly about what they like in their therapy and if you are meeting their needs."
14. What advice would you like to share about managing the anxiety that comes with starting and maintaining a practice? "Starting a private practice is not for the faint of heart. You must know how much revenue you need to bring in to offset your expenses such as rent if you have an office, malpractice insurance, office supplies (forms, business cards, etc." "Make sure you are not specializing in serving client populations that may lead to burnout, such as trauma survivors or addicts." "Be realistic with how long it will take to build a practice. Start the practice while employed elsewhere,

so you don't have to depend on the practice to pay your personal and business bills, including health insurance." "Find time to do other things when your client load drops. You may now have time to conduct insurance billing for your clients. It might mean that you'd have to take a CE course or go to the dentist or a doctor's appointment, attend a professional meeting, have lunch with a friend, file and organize your office."

15. What is the most gratifying aspect of having a private practice for you? "It's my baby. It is what I achieved, and I feel proud of the clients I have helped." "Seeing the powerful transformation of my clients in their personal and professional lives." "Being able to do what I love for work and establishing my own rules for my job." "Seeing changed lives and having clients you have helped in the past express through cards or personally sharing how you helped them." "The honor I feel when people trust me with their therapy and having the freedom to be my own businesswoman."
16. Do you have any additional recommendations or advice you would like to offer? "If you are going to build your business, you must read business and marketing books. You are the only one responsible for your practice." "Being a clinician is a very beautiful profession but can be tiresome, hard, and sad for those who don't take care of themselves, and don't set limits. It can easily consume you." "If you decide to share any personal information, make sure it is for the benefit of the client and not yourself." "Join a professional organization if you have a solo practice. Don't be afraid to be in a group practice if that fits you better than a solo practice. Don't be afraid to change."

Steven Melman, MA, LPC, LMFT

Here are my answers to the same questionnaire:

1. What degree did you obtain? MA in Clinical Psychology.
2. What licensure(s)/certification(s) have you obtained? Licensed Professional Counselor and a Licensed Marriage and Family Therapist.
3. How many total years have you been a clinician? Over 40 years.
4. What, if any, professional organizations are you a member of? Dallas Metro Counselors Association and the Relational Therapists of Dallas.
5. What is your theoretical orientation? Do you share this with your clients? CBT, along with Motivational Interviewing.
6. Are you employed, and if so, are you employed full-time or part-time? I retired from full-time employment at the end of May of 2021.
7. If you have a private practice, is it full-time or part-time? It is a part-time practice, and it always has been.
8. When you first obtained your degree and/or became licensed, did you feel confident and competent to help your clients accomplish their goals? If you didn't, approximately how long did it take you to achieve that confidence and competence? Was there anything you did to help you feel that confidence and competence? With this last question, feel free to fully elaborate. No, and that is the basis for writing this book.
9. What advice would you offer to newly licensed clinicians? Again, details will be provided in this book.

The following questions are for folks who have established and are maintaining a private practice:

1. What type of practice do you have? Do you do other things besides providing counseling, such as conducting presentations, conducting CISMs, etc.? My practice is open to seeing individuals with a variety of presenting issues, children from age 6, adolescents,

and couples. I am also contracted with insurance and EAPs to conduct presentations and CISMs.

2. If you were to start over in your private practice, is there anything you would do differently, given what you have learned through experience? No, I do not believe I would do anything differently. Looking back over my career, I think everything worked out just fine. However, I believe I needed to gain experience from employment before I considered starting a private practice. For me, I eventually decided not to enter into this venture full-time. I believed that I had the best of both worlds: having a part-time practice while a full-time employee where I received benefits: being paid for vacation and sick time and contributing to a 401 retirement.
3. From the time you became licensed, did you immediately start your practice, or were you employed elsewhere first, and if so, how long did you wait before starting your own practice? Again, I have always been employed, while my private practice was always part-time. I have had a private practice in Dallas since 1996, and at the same time, I had a practice in Commerce, TX, for 9 years.
4. How long did it take for you to establish your practice? As I recall, I had clients almost immediately in Commerce and Dallas; it perhaps took a few months before I got referrals from insurance and EAPs.
5. Do you have a specialty? No, but I am comfortable handling most issues, as you will see in subsequent chapters of this book.
6. Are you using any marketing techniques that you have found helpful that you would like to share? Initially, I had subscriptions in Dallas' Yellow Pages, but I only got a few clients from this method. So now, the only source I use is Psychology Today, and I receive a significant number of referrals.
7. What do you experience as the pros and cons of a private practice? Pros: I always wanted my own private practice; I just decided over the years that, in my case, I wanted the best of both worlds, my own business part-time while taking advantage of the benefits of being a full-time employee. Now that I am retired, I can continue

the practice that I established. It is mine, and I take great pride in the reputation I have established in the Dallas area. Cons: Having a private practice, you are always relying on the success of your marketing in obtaining clients in order to make your expenses: rent, malpractice insurance, your own health insurance, etc. And, of course, there is always the risk of a client filing a complaint against the clinician in private practice.

8. Is your practice solo, or are you part of a group practice? If you have been in both, what are the pros and cons of each? My practice has always been solo.
9. Do you contract with managed care and/or with insurance companies? If so, are a percentage of your clients coming from managed care? With insurance? Yes, I am contracted with insurance and managed care/EAPs, and the percentages are approximately 50-50. However, I occasionally have clients who do not use their insurance.
10. Do you have suggestions for setting up an office? Yes. As mentioned above by others, consider sharing office space and expenses (rent, furniture, office equipment, supplies, etc.) with a colleague to allow you to build up your practice. Also, consider transitioning from part-time to full-time. Or you can follow in my footsteps and keep your practice part-time while being employed full-time.
11. What suggestions can you offer to avoid professional burnout? I had a previous job where clinicians were required to see 35 clients in a 40-hour week, and that was required every week. I had to leave that job because I thought that would most certainly lead to my burnout. I know some colleagues in private practice who can sustain that caseload. For me, variety was the answer. As stated previously, my last job included providing counseling and conducting presentations, CISMs, etc.
12. How many clients do you typically see weekly in your practice? Now that I am retired and still have my practice, I want to keep it part-time, seeing at most 8-10 clients per week.

13. Do you have any advice you would like to share on protecting yourself from lawsuits, complicated legal issues with clients, and potential complaints to the Start Board? Yes, stay within what you are trained to practice. Don't over-promise. Be honest with clients about your role as a clinician.
14. What advice would you like to share about managing the anxiety that comes with starting and maintaining a practice? There are ebbs and flows. Sometimes, you may have an abundance of potential clients wanting to be seen, and other times you wonder when your next client will contact you for counseling. I am about to share this advice that may seem strange to you, but it has worked for me, and I don't know why. Whenever I am in need of future clients, I say out loud, "I sure could use a client or two." I don't know who is answering me, but somehow, I will start getting calls from folks requesting therapy within a day or two. Darn, if I know how that happens!
15. What is the most gratifying aspect of having a private practice for you? As long as I have thought of my career aspirations, they have been to help clients improve their lives, marriages, etc. And having a private practice that is mine to accomplish those goals is so satisfying and gratifying!
16. Do you have any additional recommendations or advice you would like to offer? Many other suggestions and advice will be further addressed in this book.

Additional Advice To The /New Clinician

I saw this article from the December 2022 Psychology Today publication. The composition was entitled "The 7 Traits of A Great Therapist" by Abigail Fagan. The seven traits are trust-building, open-mindedness, inquiring, demand accountability, versatility, unifying, and self-aware. Much of the information in the article solidifies my beliefs about the traits of a great therapist.

Trust-building: Clients can only feel comfortable revealing their vulnerabilities and fears, but only if they "feel completely safe and unjudged." "Research shows that the effectiveness of therapy hinges on the therapeutic alliance-the relationship between the therapist and the patient." The author states that great therapists' curiosity creates trust-building. "Great therapists are fascinated by the variety of human experience and are eager to discover more about the individual sitting before them." She continues, "A second element of rapport is listening attentively. Establishing therapy as an enterprise in which the patient feels completely heard, forges a special connection between the two of you." The third component of rapport is non-judgmentalism, "which frees the patient to open up and allows the therapist to take in who the person is."

She concludes that the three elements are essential in establishing rapport. Then once established, "the rapport is continually being nurtured." She further states, "Rapport may be strengthened by a dash of self-disclosure by the therapist in response to a pertinent question. It may be sustained by voicing optimism about the patient's ability to change." She quotes Noam Shapancer, a clinical psychologist and professor of psychology at Otterbein University, "As long as rapport is there, you can recover from setbacks or mistakes."

Open-minded: The author, Ms. Fagan, quotes Daniel Marston, a Pennsylvania psychologist, "Great therapists don't begin with a fixed point of view about what the outcome should be. They are guided by the patient and the patient's view of a meaningful life." The therapist's role is to help the client achieve their goals and to make the patient the best they can be, not the person the therapist thinks they should be." That would include the counseling of couples. Many clinicians believe they know what a healthy romantic relationship should resemble and want to impart their opinion on the couples' goals in having a successful relationship. The article gave the example of a couple struggling with the possibility of living apart for a period before marrying. As a couple's therapist, the author cautioned against having pre-conceived beliefs that long-distance relationships cannot survive. The therapist's role in this example is to help the couple achieve the goal of living apart for a finite period while keeping the relationship intact.

Inquiring: Ms. Fagan states that "Probing questions helps the therapist understand patients and patients understand themselves." The therapist uses their "creativity and wisdom" in their questions. There isn't a perfect way to use the inquiry process, but a great therapist uses both compassion and kindness. The author emphasizes the "Why Now" in the inquiry process. It is essential that every clinician add that into their line of questions in an intake interview. I also have incorporated the "why now" by asking clients, "What led you to seek counseling now?" "Was there a precipitating event that made you request counseling now?" Sometimes, male clients will state that their wife threatened divorce if they didn't agree to marital therapy. Or it could be that their supervisor threatened to terminate their employment if they didn't get help with their alcohol abuse. Also, through the inquiry process, a great therapist will use their creativity by asking questions that make the client consider alternative ways of examining their issue and, thus, alternative methods of resolving their presenting problem.

Continuing with the discussion of the inquiry process, Ms. Kagan again quotes Noam Shpancer regarding the "habit of avoidance," such as pain. Dr. Shpancer states, "People develop a habit of avoidance because it worked in the short term, but that habit can become the problem in the long term." Therefore, the wise clinician will ask the client what they are avoiding by continuing to exhibit their current behavior. Another question the clinician can ask is if you stop the problematic behavior, what will you be losing or what will you be gaining? He further elaborated, "Probing questions help patients understand their avoidance and take action to break free. Incisive questions can be revelatory,"

Demand Accountability: In addition to using empathy with their clients, great therapists also hold them accountable. Ms. Fagan says Dr. Shapancer, like me, also uses cognitive behavioral therapy (CBT) and implements "cognitive reappraisal is the ability to examine the validity of their thoughts." For instance, if a client uses all-or-nothing statements, a clinician can ask the client what evidence they have to support their statements. If they don't have any proof, the therapist helps the patient learn to challenge those thoughts or statements that fall into the realm of negative self-talk. Other techniques that can be used to hold clients accountable are role reversal and exposure, such as working with a client who has anxiety or obsessive-compulsive disorder symptoms. Exposure to them helps build up their confidence in overcoming a stated fear. Dr. Shapancer gave examples of helping one client who feared meeting new peers in college and another who had been in a car accident.

Versatile: Great therapists are adaptable. If one technique isn't effective, they are not afraid to use another. Psychiatrist Mark Rego, a clinical assistant professor at the Yale School of Medicine, advises clinicians "not to be a one-trick pony."

Unifying: This relates to the counseling of couples. The author, Ms. Fagan, emphasizes, "Great couples therapists take on a leadership role to unify a couple's goals." The example offered in the article was the wife who said she wanted more emotional support from her husband. The husband said he wanted more sex from his wife. The wise clinician "identifies each partner's needs, then leads the couple in conversation to help them discover it for themselves by asking questions, reflecting back what is heard, synthesizing the two perspectives and checking whether the insight is aligned with both partners."

Self-awareness: What makes a great therapist is their self-awareness, which is essential to being an effective clinician. An excellent therapist has a deep understanding of who they are. They are comfortable in their own skin. They are aware of their biases and prejudices and do their best to keep them outside their counseling office. They are aware of their "own assumptions, especially about cultural differences, gender, and race, says Los Angeles psychologist Jennice Vilhauer." They are comfortable asking clients to educate the clinician about their culture, religion, and family traditions. The example given is the "good therapist might ask the patient, what are your thoughts about why your parents want you to do that? -which may unearth cultural norms that can then be openly discussed in light of what the patient believes is a healthy dynamic. Such an approach helps the therapist identify how to move forward and reduces resistance from the patient who might have otherwise dismissed the guidance." Finally, this section suggests that a great therapist recognizes when a patient may need to be referred to another clinician. Ms. Fagan concludes her article by saying, "A great therapist may not be a great therapist for every patient-but every patient can, with time, find a great therapist."

Assessment & Progress Notes

As clinicians, we are taught many different ways to document an assessment from my many clinical jobs over the years. When I decided to begin my private practice, I began using a 2-page evaluation that meets my needs in assessing a client, couple, or family.

The assessment includes the following: "The Participants," their ages and if it consists of the child, what grade they are in, and school they attend; "Presenting Problem" and the details (what is occurring now, for how long, how they began, symptoms, and how it is impacting the client, marriage or family); "Family Issues (Present and Past)" and this would include the family of origin, how many years a couple has been married, number of children, their ages, their relationships with family members, etc. and include all pertinent info; "Medical/Psychiatric Issues (Present and Past)," which would consist of physical health, psychiatric health, medications they take, dosages and frequency (and if they are successful in controlling the symptoms), any psychiatric details about hospitalizations; "Previous Counseling" include whether the counseling was helpful or not and the whys; "Mental Status," "Substance Abuse Issues (Present and Past,)" and again include all details with client, couple and family of origin; "Other Significant Information" "Client or Couple's Goals" which could consist of your suggestions to the client if they fail to address any; "(Your) Clinical Impressions:" "Counseling Intervention" you are going to provide, such as individual, marital, family counseling; "(Any) Counseling Goals" that are different or in addition to the client's goals. Regarding this Intake Assessment Form, feel free to adopt one that meets your needs with your clients. As I complete the intake on paper, I am mindful of how important it is to protect my clients from disclosing too much information should their records ever be subpoenaed. I am also cognizant of what I put in their records should the clients request a copy of their chart.

In the same way, I want to address the use of Progress Notes. I have used many notes over the years in working with numerous employers, including SOAP (Subjective, Objective, Assessment, Progress/Plan) Notes). Over the years in private practice, I have adopted using progress notes that summarize how the client is doing since the last session, any changes since their previous appointment, what was discussed or addressed during the current session, what homework or assignment is given for the next session and the date of the next meeting. My notes, including the Intake Assessment, are designed to assist me and are devoid of any diagnoses, biases, or psychological jargon. Again, I am always mindful when writing my notes about how they would be viewed by an attorney or in a court of law. I want to keep my progress notes short and to the point. The progress note should provide me with a summary of what has occurred in each session and the direction and goals that were agreed upon by the clinician and the client. Finally, they should be written so that a fellow clinician could pick up the chart and continue where I have left off.

When I began seeing clients in my first clinical job, I was so stiff and almost mechanical, robotic, without much emotion or displaying my personality. In my mind, I said to myself that clients are coming for counseling for serious issues, and I need to treat them accordingly. A colleague at the time gave me wise advice. He suggested that I will be a better therapist when I am able to bring my personality and my sense of humor into my counseling sessions. So, I began incorporating that recommendation into my spiel to clients: "I take very seriously that brings you to counseling, and I want you to know that I equally take them seriously. I know how hard it was for you to call and initiate therapy. But at the same time, I am providing counseling to you; I want you to enjoy the process, including laughing and each of us bringing our personalities into each session. In addition, I want you to be able to tell family members and friends (if you choose to) that yes, you are going to counseling, and not only has it been very beneficial, but "we (my counselor and I have fun at the same time."

When you are conducting an intake, engage in a conversation with your clients by asking questions. Over the years, I have continued to remind myself to listen and ask questions before intervening. I start my every intake by asking each new client the same question: "What brings you to counseling: how can I be of assistance to you?" This has been reinforced by clients, who have complimented me for allowing them to fully divulge their presenting issues. I only interrupt when I need to ask questions for clarification or obtain additional information. I always ask clients what goals they want to achieve. My mental image is imagining the clients' issues as jigsaw pieces spread out on a table. Together, you and your client are engaging collaboratively to put the pieces together that accomplish the client's goals. I tell clients that I try to paint mental pictures for them. I have learned that the best way for them to grasp what I am trying to convey is by having them visualize it. So, I tell clients that my challenge is how to verbally say things to them logically in the same way I thought it through in my head first.

It is okay to use the collaborative approach if the client disagrees with your hypothesis or conclusion, whether during the intake or in any subsequent session. If that should happen, you, the clinician, can ask the client to educate you on how your conclusions were inaccurate. Not only is this approach indicative of collaboration, but it also lets the client know that you want the client's input. You, the clinician, can use the phrase, "Well, help me to understand you and see it differently; I may have misinterpreted what you were trying to convey."

I also want to take the mystique out of counseling, and I want clients to say, "Well, that makes sense." When it comes to conversing with clients, relate to them on their level, not trying to impress them with big words or jargon or with your education. One factor in success with your adult clients is to relate to them equally, whether they have advanced education or never graduated from high school. You want the client to believe they are heard and understood, and you convey empathy in connecting with their emotional pain.

So, again, the essence of my counseling stance is through the use of CBT (Cognitive-Behavioral Therapy) and MI (Motivational Interviewing) to help clients and couples accomplish their goals. I do not dictate what clients or couples should do. It is their life and their relationship if they are seeking couples counseling. However, I will ask thought-provoking questions and gently challenge irrational or contradictory thoughts. I never want a client or a couple to feel like they are being picked on or to have them become defensive. And I purposely asked them if they thought I was picking on them. If they thought I had, then I apologized and changed the therapeutic direction.

There is another issue to consider and for you, as a therapist, to decide, and that is how many clients you are comfortable seeing in a day and a week. You need to answer this question, especially if providing counseling is not just a job in the short term but one that will sustain you over your career. I once worked at a counseling center, where in the beginning, there weren't any requirements to see a certain number of clients per day, per week, or per month. Then, the two owners of the company sold to a large corporation. It became a nightmare for us, the clinicians. Eventually, it became a requirement that the therapist would be expected to see 35 clients in a 40-hour week, and seven of the 35 clients would be new clients every week. I have always seen new clients throughout my career for longer than an hour. My supervisor, in that setting, said if I were to see new clients longer than an hour, I would need to work more than 40 hours a week. I asked this supervisor which was more important, the number of clients seen or the quality of services to the clients. Of course, her reply was both. I believed these requirements of seeing so many clients every week would lead to eventual burnout. Over time, I concluded that I was comfortable seeing no more than three clients in a row and then having a break before seeing again no more than an additional 3 in a row.

Some clinicians in private practice are very comfortable seeing more than eight clients daily. Equally, they are content with having 40 or more clients on their caseload. Again, my private practice has always been part-time, but if it were full-time and when I was employed, I would not want to see more than six clients daily. So, every therapist, whether in private practice or employed, must arrive at these answers for themselves: the number of clients on their caseload and how many clients they are comfortable seeing each day and each week without experiencing burnout. Again, as mentioned earlier in this chapter, some clinicians need variety. They enjoy providing counseling, but their practice is also sustained by teaching, consulting, etc. Again, in my case, I had the best of both worlds: I had a part-time private practice while also employed, where I conducted presentations, account management, management consultations, CISMs (Critical Incident Stress Management), etc.

The previous paragraph was all about finding out what works for you in taking care of yourself. So, as you determine how many clients you want to see in a day, it would be healthy to consider sticking with the 50 minutes or an hour for return clients. You would want to have noted in your Statement of Understanding or the Consent to Treat form that clients would sign that their sessions are 50 minutes long. This form, whatever name you call it, must be signed by every client before therapy commences. Again, the only times I exceeded the 50-minute hour were when conducting the intake or if a return client was in a crisis. I prided myself on being punctual with my clients. I saw them on time at their appointment time. Keeping to the 50 minutes or an hour would allow me to write or type that client's progress note and prepare for your next client. The same thing I say to clients applies to us as clinicians. We must determine how to best take care of ourselves, and once we arrive at how to do that, we should rarely deviate!

Again, as I write this book, I have provided therapy for more than 40 years. Except for the first 3 years (when I lived and worked in Wichita Falls, I have spent the rest of my career in Dallas.) Wherever I have worked, whether employed or in private practice, it has always been critical to how others viewed me. My reputation with colleagues, clients, and Federal agency Points of Contact (POCs) has always guided me towards excellence and to be the best I can be in whatever role I am providing. My various roles have included counseling, conducting presentations, management consultations, CISMs, working with a mental health judge, and helping colleagues acquire skills to feel confident and competent.

I use the following exercise on myself and with my clients, and you are more than welcome to try it yourself. First, take a sheet of paper and write down how you perceive yourself by noting your attributes. Then, ask yourself if you believe others perceive you similarly. Lastly, ask those you trust to give you feedback if there is a match between your perceptions of yourself and how others perceive you.

As I have completed the exercise by noting my attributes and then asking for feedback, these are the attributes that are most important to me (in no particular order): dependability, resourcefulness, trustworthiness, ability to get along with almost everyone (including clients who are requesting therapy), good listening skills and the ability to simplify and put my words into everyday language.

These attributes have served me well in helping clients achieve their goals. In addition, I want former clients to recommend me to their friends and family members. Finally, I would like to obtain referrals from colleagues, insurance, and managed care companies because of the reputation I have earned over these many decades.

I hope the attributes you listed will help propel you to success and that you find the career you have chosen as rewarding as it has been for me. The rest of the book will be devoted to sharing strategies and techniques that I successfully applied while working with different client populations and their presenting issues. There will be other instances where my goal and purpose are to be thought-provoking, perhaps challenging your views on certain subjects, and even provocative at times.

CHAPTER 3:

The Counseling and Education of Our Children and Adolescents

ESTABLISHING A RAPPORT with adults is crucial, so connecting with the child or adolescent from the initial first impression is essential. You may not get another chance to see them again if you were unsuccessful in making that connection. To succeed with these populations, I try to put myself into the age of the child or adolescent I see. As clinicians and parents, we have the ability to recall what it was like to be at a younger age and what a child's or adolescent's thought processes are.

When providing counseling to children, you need to know your limitations. For instance, I do not counsel any child younger than the age of 6. I would refer those children to a play therapist because I do not have that specialty or credentials. I am especially cautious about the diagnosis I give to children, adolescents, and adults, especially when submitting a diagnosis to insurance or managed care companies. I will often provide the most benign diagnosis that is accurate but with less labeling to the client I am serving. I may share symptoms with the client and ask if the client can relate to those symptoms. In the client's chart of record that I keep, I may assign a diagnosis that I believe is accurate but submit the more benign one to insurance companies or managed care. Again, I go back to when I was an adolescent and psychologists' diagnoses of me and their detrimental predictions.

When counseling parents, I often suggest they avoid verbal battles with their child or adolescent. Instead, I tell these parents to remind themselves what it was like to be at their current offspring's age. When they can achieve this task, they can then consider the motivation of their child or adolescent's behavior. At the same time, the parents can tell themselves what they expect from their child and plan their behavior accordingly to guide the child to their expectations. It is a balancing act between the parents guiding or molding their child or adolescent towards the desired behavior and simultaneously listening to their offspring's viewpoint. Parents should encourage a dialogue with their child or adolescent. Parents need to be able to explain the rationale behind their request or perspective. One of the biggest mistakes some parents make is not to provide any rationale or explanation. Instead, they will tell their child, "Because I told you to" or "because I said so". How can the child understand what is behind the parents' request based on what the parent just said? If the child or adolescent can understand the parent's reason, they may accept the explanation and abide by the parent's request. Another mistake some parents are guilty of is trying to be their child or adolescent's friend rather than their parent.

Continuing my dialogue with parents, I inform them that we are all mortals and will not live forever. So, our role as parents is to provide them with tools, strategies, and the ability to problem-solve. Parents can look at their child's age, whether teenager or young adult and decide what traits and lessons they still need to pass on to their offspring to be successful in the world while these parents are still alive.

Let me offer this scenario that teaches children morals by presenting challenging dilemmas. Let's say that an elderly individual dropped a $20 bill in front of the child. The parent would ask the child what they would do. The child could imagine what they would do with $20, but the parent could ask the child that perhaps the older person needed the $20 for medication or groceries. The point of this exercise is to present the two choices and have the child make the right choice by informing the older person that they dropped their money and give it back to them.

Here is another dilemma, but this one is directed at adolescents. Suppose a parent encouraged their adolescent to call them if they need a ride home, no matter what time of night it is. Now, the adolescent's friend had driven them to a party, and unbeknownst to the teen, there was alcohol at the party, and the friend and driver had become intoxicated. In questioning their teen, the parents wanted to present the challenge to their offspring. Does the teen take a chance and allow their inebriated friend to bring them back home or call the parent and ask them to pick them up? Again, the parent wanted to present this dilemma to the adolescent and ask them what they would do. Hopefully, the teen would say they would call home, and hopefully, the parent would agree to pick them up without referencing the lateness of the hour or how much their sleep might be interrupted. This paragraph and the previous one have a lot in common to offer the child and adolescent scenarios and get each of them to make the right choices. The purpose of these exercises is to make them think and problem-solve while the parents are alive, and this process can be utilized long after the parents have departed.

The following is a strategy and scenario to use with parents. A parent takes their 5-year-old to the grocery store. Unfortunately, the mother or father takes the child down the candy aisle, naturally, the child states, they want candy. The parent may make the situation worse when they say no. The child throws themselves to the floor and begins a temper tantrum. Lord helps the parent who sees other shoppers staring and gives in to the child's desires. It is as if the child is taking an index finger and moving it down as if to say, "Got ya!" Imagine, if you will, the child is on stage, and the parent is part of the audience, and the child is saying, "This performance is for you." To break the temper tantrum, the parent could instead leave the child and walk to the end of the aisle and round the corner. The parent can still see the child, but the child cannot see the parent. The child will notice their parent has left them. The child will interrupt their tantrum to find the parent. When the child does find the parent, the parent can then respond in this way. "I am so glad you are here with me. Would you help me shop? I don't know what I would do if you were not here to help me." The parent has successfully provided a distraction from focusing on the candy and bolstered the child's self-esteem by telling their child their assistance is needed.

Children from an early age want to be helpful, and it is the wise parent who takes advantage of the child's desires. Therefore, the parent can encourage the child to help set the table, even if at age 3, getting them to carry napkins and silverware to be placed around the plates. As the child ages, parents can encourage them to stir a pot, help them cook or bake, or help with yard work, etc. Parents will find that if they involve children early on with their natural desire to help, they will have teenagers conditioned to be involved with family tasks.

Along with getting children and adolescents involved in household chores, it is also vital to praise them for every wanted behavior. Even we, as adults, want to be acknowledged and praised by others (our spouse or a supervisor), whether it is a task completed at work or home. Children and adolescents are no different. For all of us, it increases our self-esteem and pride in completing tasks and goals and having those endeavors acknowledged and appreciated by others.

There has been much discussion and debate about whether competition should be introduced and maintained or eliminated with children and adolescents. I believe competition helps children and adolescents to strive to do their best. Without it, there is no incentive, and there is no bar to try to exceed. When children and adolescents become adults, there certainly is competition, so learning about and understanding this concept at an early age will help them to accept it as adults. For the life of me, I don't know why adults and even some healthcare professionals have an issue with the concept of competition regarding our youth. It is undoubtedly present in sports, from children's to professional sports. When we cheer on our favorite sports team or are selected amongst other candidates for a job or promotion, it is indicative of competition.

Let's talk about school grades. Grades are one way that indicates how well a child or adolescent understands how successful they have been in learning a particular subject. I know and accept this. However, there aren't grades when we enter the work world. So, I offer a concept to children and adolescents to do their best, whether in school, at work, or in life in general. I will, for instance, ask a child or an adolescent if they did their best on a test. I will remind them that doing their best is tempered and balanced with the other courses they are taking. I will share with them my own example; there were several classes in college I wished I had done better. But at the same time, I had other courses, their assignments, and tests to pass.

The same can be said in the working world. We have more than one task to achieve in a given day, so one cannot expect perfection on any particular task. Perfection is just a myth, anyway. So, we are always trying to balance our best and letting go of the concept of perfection because perfection is not achievable. Therefore, I always tell all my clients that no one can ask any more than our best, including yourself. And one's best having to be spread out over one's other responsibilities. So again, I encourage children and adolescents to put forth their best effort in school, household tasks, and, eventually, the jobs they will hold.

So, in summary, parents need to strike a balance between encouraging their offspring to be their best without exerting too much pressure on them to do well in school and allowing them to still be kids. Parents should not put extreme stress on their dependents and should only accept them if they get straight As, get into the most prestigious schools, or choose the most lucrative professions.

Parents might also put undue pressure on their kids to be the best in sports or play a musical instrument. But, again, there needs to be a balance between encouragement and allowing the child or adolescent to have fun while acquiring new skills. Parents need to resist the temptation to constantly pressure kids to practice and perform near-perfect expectations.

When these parents put enormous pressure on their kids, they may observe them experiencing problems with their sleep and may exhibit symptoms of anxiety and depression and a decrease or loss of self-esteem. In addition, the constant stress to perform causes them to feel like they're not good enough or that they will never be good enough. Finally, when the emphasis is on achievement rather than learning, the child or adolescent may resort to cheating. It could be cheating on a test, paying someone to write their term paper, or taking a college entrance test for them.

So, what are some solutions that parents and their children or adolescents can do? First, the parent and the offspring can use encouragement to do their best. Focus on the process rather than the end result. If the parent puts so much pressure on their child, they can ask themselves why their performance, test score, or success are so important. Second, the parent can ask the child to verbalize what they are trying to achieve or its importance to them. Third, the parent should allow the child or adolescent to share their thoughts and feelings rather than interjecting theirs onto their offspring. Allowing the child or adolescent to be heard will encourage them rather than have them feel they have disappointed the parent.

I often try to think of innovative ways of working with and counseling children and adolescents. It is imperative to earn their trust, for them to see me as being different from their parents and that I am not there to take the side of their parents. So, as a way of establishing rapport with a young client, I may tell some juvenile jokes, such as this one: "A teacher is trying to teach her class, but a loud noise drowns her out. Little Johnny is in the back row, using his attached desk chair as his racecar. The noise he is making is the sound of a racecar being shifted and tires squealing as he imagines his racecar is going around the track. The teacher identifies Johnny as the source of the noise and yells, 'Johnny, stop.' Johnny then makes the noise of a racecar, whose brakes are being applied hard and tires screeching as the imaginary car abruptly stops."

Here is another joke I sometimes tell. "A teacher has assigned a project for each student to work on in class. She goes up and down the aisle, ensuring each student understands and completes the task. In the meantime, little Johnny is busy drawing a spaceship, and he is proud of his accomplishment. As the teacher approaches Johnny's desk, she notices his drawing, takes it off his desk, and begins to crumple up his picture. Johnny whispers into an imaginary microphone and says, 'Ahh, Houston, we've got a problem!'"

Once upon a time, I was an instructor of a college class helping first-year students succeed in college. The individual who oversaw the instructors of this course required us to teach the students how to juggle. I asked her how I could teach them how to juggle if I didn't know. Then, her reply was, "I guess you will have to learn." So, it was a challenge for me to learn how to juggle. As I struggled to learn, I remember using the word "can't" repeatedly. I soon realized that I had to eliminate that word from my vocabulary if I was going to master the task of juggling.

Sometimes in session, I will also teach children and adolescent clients how to juggle beanbags. First, I show them how I can juggle all three beanbags at once and then ask them to do the same. Of course, they tell me they don't know how. So, I informed them that juggling was nothing more than tossing and catching; if they could toss and catch, they could learn this feat. But it is learning how to juggle all three simultaneously was the challenge. If they state the task is too complex, I explain the self-fulfilling prophecy; once we say something is hard, it becomes hard, and now we have two obstacles to overcome. Not only does the individual still need to learn how to juggle, but now they need to overcome them, having used the word "can't" or that the task is just "too hard."

Once they have learned how to juggle, I explained the reason behind my teaching them the task by saying, "From now on, whatever you are learning, whether it is a foreign language or calculus, do not tell yourself that you can't learn something or the task is too hard. But instead, just like juggling, if you break the enormous task into smaller ones, where each step is predicated on the previous one, then the overall goal can be achieved." I recently heard a saying that seems relevant. "Things are hard before they become easy." This example of learning how to juggle can be applied to any other challenge. This example will again pertain to me. After I have completed writing and publishing this book, my next challenge is my long-long dream of learning how to play the guitar. I wish I had learned when I was younger.

When I begin counseling a child, if focusing on the issue is the target of a bull's eye, I start at the periphery, asking the child all kinds of questions to establish that essential rapport, including telling those juvenile jokes. For other examples, I inquire about their favorite school subjects and why, what subjects they wish they didn't have to take, their interests, whether they have friends and siblings, how they get along with them and their parents, etc. Whatever questions I can think of in an effort to build a rapport with these young clients. Feel free to use any techniques to help you connect with and establish a counseling relationship with your pre-adult clients. For example, as I tell an age-appropriate joke, I will ask a child if they have a joke they would like to share with me. Likewise, if they want to draw, I will ask them if they would like to draw a picture for me.

If we want our children and adolescents to be the best they can be, then I need to bring the next issue to your attention, and that topic is being debated in the United States. Is our education system today equal to that of previous generations? According to the Business Insider report in 2018, education in the US was ranked 38th in math scores and 24th in science. But once upon a time in America, when farming was more predominant in the US, some folks only had an 8th-grade education. So, I wonder if our current and past high school graduates could pass the 8th-grade final exam that was given in 1895 from Salina, Kansas. The following excerpt questions came from the Genealogical

Society and Library and were reprinted by the Salina Journal. I also added some of my own questions, and both are noted below:

Grammar

Give 9 rules for the use of Capital Letters.

What are the Principal Parts of a verb? Give examples and differences between lay and lie.

Write a composition of about 150 words and show therein that you understand the practical use of the rules of grammar.

Arithmetic

Name and define the Fundamentals Rules of Arithmetic.

A wagon box is 2 ft deep, 10 ft long, and is 3 ft wide. How many bushels of wheat will it hold?

District 33 has a valuation of $35,000. What is the necessary levy to carry on a school 7 months at $50 per month and have $104 for incidentals?

Find the cost of 6720 lbs. of coal at $6.00 per ton.

Find the interest of $512.60 for 8 months and 18 days at 7 percent.

Find a bank discount of $300 for 90 days (no grace) at 10 percent.

Write a Bank Check, a Promissory Note, and a Receipt.

US History

Give an account of the discovery of America by Columbus.

Relate the causes and results of the Revolutionary War.

Relate the causes and results of the Civil War.

Relate the causes and results of World War I.

Relate the causes and results of World War II.

Name the events connected with the following dates: 1492, 1861, 1865, (In the future beyond 1895, I could include additional years such as 1914-1919, 1929, 1940-1945, 1963, 1968, and 9/11/2001.

Geography

What is climate? Upon what does climate depend?

How do we account for the extremes of climate in the US and the World?

Of what use are rivers? Of what use are oceans?

Name some of the mountains in the US.

I could add an addendum to the test by asking students to find these places on a map: Iran, North Korea, Vietnam, Great Britain, Greece, Israel, Illinois, Wyoming, and Rhode Island.

Other addendum questions: Name the capitals of all the US states, name all the capitals in Europe,

Why is the Atlantic Coast colder than the Pacific at the same latitude?

Describe the process by which the water of an ocean returns to the sources of rivers.

Students taking the 1895 Salina test were given 6 hours to complete it.

Here are additional questions I would ask today's students:

Civics

What is the Bill of Rights?

Tell as much as you know about the US Constitution. Why is it essential that the Constitution be followed as written and intended by the forefathers?

How many House of Representative seats are there?

How many US Senators are there?

How are presidents elected, and why is the Electoral College still relevant and vital in electing our presidents?

What are the roles of the Legislative, Executive, and Judicial branches of government?

Again, some of the questions came from me, especially in the area of civics. I do not believe that our schools teach civics as they once did. Instead, I contend that the emphasis needs to be on teaching the Constitution as intended by the writers and signers of the Constitution. We need to follow those principles. After all, the Constitution and the Bill of Rights, written by our forefathers, wanted to make this country different from every other one in the world. And I believe it is a disservice to our students that they are not taught civics as they were in previous generations.

Currently, there is another debate on how US history should be taught to students. One group of educators and maybe even politicians believe that if parts of our history make students (and even adults) uncomfortable, it should be avoided and not taught at all. Therefore, textbooks must include all historical events and debated issues (Capitalism vs Socialism, whether global warming, climate change, or extreme weather is settled science or just theories, etc.). I saw a bumper sticker that I thought was effective, "It's not politics, it's history." All history ought to be taught. I recently saw this quote from Lieutenant Colonel Allen West that is worth noting, "History is not there for you to like or dislike. It's there for you to learn from it. And if it offends you, even better. Because then you are less likely to repeat it. It is not yours to erase or destroy; it belongs to all of us." If I had my way, US history would be divided into segments, and each segment would be taught from the 9th grade to the 12th. And, of course, they will be taught civics before high school students graduate.

There has been some debate about whether the Department of Education and Common Core have improved children's education in reading, math, and science in the United States and in comparison to other countries. But before you arrive at your own conclusions, I believe you need information about Common Core.

The following came from an article from the sites of Penn State University, entitled "Common Core: What Is It and Why Is It So Controversial?" on January 28, 2016. The author states, "Common Core is the government's attempt at standardizing what is taught across our country. The Common Core State Standards define what a student should know by each grade. They are not meant to provide a day-by-day curriculum for a teacher but rather a general basis for a year-long curriculum. U.S. News discusses the differences between the old standards and the Common Core as differences in rigor and more evaluative problem-solving." I agree with the author that educating our children and adolescents is to teach them how to read and acquire math and science skills.

However, an article by Punjab Colleges entitled "Everything You Need To Know About; What Is Common Core Education? What Is Social Education In Education? What Is Equity In Education?" I agree with the notion in the article that educators need to teach students to develop cognitive thinking, acquire mathematical skills, and develop logical thinking. Where I disagree is the emphasis on teaching students about social justice, injustices, and inequities. There is enough on the plate of educators to teach students how to think, not what to think. The author stated that learning about social justice may lead students to be "overcome with reactions of guilt, disapproval or resentment to reach an active commitment to promoting justice and equality at all levels: personal, institutional, national or global." And how were these reactions derived in the first place? Maybe they were imprinted by liberal educators?

Here is another example of how a thesis, called the 1619 Project, has been accepted by liberal journalists and academia. The 1619 Project was created by New York Times Magazine reporter Nikole Hannah-Jones in August 2019. The project has been taken as gospel by these liberal institutions and is now taught in high schools and universities. The central premise of this project is that America was founded not in 1776 but in 1619, and the Revolutionary War was fought to preserve slavery. It doesn't matter how many historians have opposed the author's allegations in print; the 1619 Project is still considered accurate by those whose intentions are to rewrite history. Another point the project emphasizes is that America still must be seen through the lens of slavery. That view of America is the original sin that can never be overcome. They believe every black person today is a victim of America's original sin from 1619.

Instead of embracing the 1619 Project and accepting the fallacies of this theory in our education system, I believe students should be told that the United States is where they want to be to make something of themselves, where they can achieve their hopes and dreams. Even if racism does exist, this is the best place in the world to overcome it. In the US, each person can define their future. Look at all the examples of blacks and other minorities who experienced racism and other challenges and overcame them. We have more opportunities in this country compared to others. Do not squander those opportunities. Stop believing that we can't achieve them as a society and that only the government can assist us. Former President Ronald Reagan, at a press conference on August 12th, 1986, said it well, "The nine most terrifying words in the English language are: I am from the federal government, and I am here to help."

Here is something else to ponder that I recently heard. Consider that there is no such thing as race. Instead, accept culture as an alternative to race. There are different cultures in the US and around the world. Some cultures do good things while other cultures don't. We can change cultures. We can judge cultures. But culture has little to do with race. For example, some folks would say those who have lived in New Orleans for generations have a particular culture. They are not of a specific race but share similarities regarding food and the influence of other countries that once occupied New Orleans. Another example would be inhabitants from the countries of Mexico, Spain, Puerto Rico, and South America. Each person from each country speaks different Spanish dialects, but one would not refer to them as being of the same race; they are from different cultures or ethnicities.

Recently, a survey was sent to me that I want to share with you. I will offer my comments after you have had a chance to read the:

SOCIALISM IN AMERICA SURVEY

1. Do you believe that the phrase "democratic socialism" is nothing more than just "socialism"?
   YES or NO
2. Do you believe that capitalism — not socialism — is the best path to human flourishing, equality, and justice for all?
   YES or NO
3. How concerned are you that young Americans across the country are being persuaded toward socialism?
   VERY CONCERNED
   NOT CONCERNED AT ALL
4. Do you believe the American education system has failed to properly communicate the threat socialism poses to American founding principles to students?

YES or NO

5. How important is it to expand the understanding young people have of limited government, economic freedom, and the rule of law found in America's founding principles?
   VERY IMPORTANT
   NOT THAT IMPORTANT
6. How important is it to reach high school students with programs that teach core free-market economic principles and contrast them to socialism for students?
   VERY IMPORTANT
   NOT THAT IMPORTANT
7. How important is it to give teachers the resources, support, and teaching materials that they need to promote free-market economics to their students in K-12 education?
   VERY IMPORTANT
   NOT THAT IMPORTANT
8. What other thoughts would you like to share with us today regarding socialism?

I am sharing this survey with you as this is the current debate in this country. Again, this is an example of how our educators of high schoolers and college and the media are brainwashing the public about socialism over capitalism. But before I proceed any further, let me share some truths about socialism. Socialism is a system that ensures members of society get their fair share (as determined by the government), and the government must be able to control property, production, and distribution.

Former President Ronald Reagan, in a 60 Minutes interview with Mike Wallace in 1975, used the word Fascism in place of Socialism. "What is Fascism? Fascism is private ownership and private enterprise but with total government control and regulation. If Fascism ever comes to America, it will come in the name of liberalism." As a result of Socialism or Fascism, there is less entrepreneurial opportunity. There is either limited or non-existent competition, and the consequence is a lack of motivation by individuals. This causes lesser rewards, a reduced incentive to work, and reduced prosperity. The state or federal government is responsible for its citizens' basic necessities of life. There is a limited choice and sometimes a shortage of consumer products, and the prices for goods are fixed. There is an emphasis on equality for all, but at the same time, there is no reward for individuals to go above and beyond what is expected of them. This, of course, can lead to complacency.

Those in support of socialism state that there are no universal truths, only injustices occurring throughout the world. Today, the currently accepted term is "political modernist," which used to be referred to as Marxism. With the political modernist, there is an assault on dialogue, reason, rationale, scientific method, truth, and critical thinking. Everything is seen from the lens of race. This way of thinking has been referred to as a "mind virus."

But it isn't just the government ownership of businesses and production. Examples of those advocating socialism in the US want to cancel all student debt or introduce free college for everyone. The only problem with this thinking is, who will pay for the cancellation of student debt or the free college? There is no such thing as free college. The only way to pay for it is through higher taxes. If the cancellation of student debt were to occur, it would be paid for by either those who have never gone to college or those who are paying off their own debt or have done so in the past. And, of course, college tuition will not decrease, so the current cost will only rise with each generation. In my opinion, the price of college (tuition, books, etc.) dramatically increased when the federal government took over the student loan program. When I obtained my Master's degree in 1980, I took out a student loan at a cost of about $5000 for my first semester. After securing that loan for that semester, I decided I did not want to incur any more debt, So I applied and was hired full-time as a counselor at a boys' home for juvenile delinquents while I was a full-time graduate student. I am not sure how to bring down the cost of college education, but I do know the answer is not "free college," as endorsed by today's socialist politicians. Former British Prime Minister Margaret Thatcher had a very appropriate quote, "The problem with socialism is that you eventually run out of other peoples' money."

I saw this quote from Gerald L. K. Smith, who had written the passage in his magazine, "The Cross and the Flag," in 1942, "You cannot legislate the poor into freedom by legislating the wealthy out of freedom. What one person receives without working for, another person must work for without receiving. The government cannot give anybody anything that it does not first take from somebody else. When half of the people get the idea that they do not have to work because the other half is going to take care of them, and when the other half gets the idea that it does no good to work because somebody else is going to get what they worked for, that, my dear friend, is the end of any nation. You cannot multiply wealth by dividing it."

Fifty years ago, it would have been unthinkable to consider socialism over capitalism in this country. Who would have imagined that some would try to persuade us that socialism is a better form of government for us than what our forefathers envisioned? A country founded on freedom, limited government, and government officials working for the American people, not the other way around. Yet, we (especially children, adolescents, and young adults) are being brainwashed that socialism is the solution to our problems by some politicians, the news media, and some of our educators.

In a later chapter, I will discuss the concepts of Diversity, Equity, and Inclusion, currently referred to as DEI. Still, I want to address how diversity is not occurring on college campuses as it relates to university professors. It may seem apparent that for those who espouse diversity, whether on college campuses or in business or government, emphasizing diversity amongst races or cultures is essential. But diversity in thoughts and beliefs will not be tolerated. Everyone must drink the same Kool-Aid. Below is a graph showing how university instructors were liberal in 1989 and how it has become even more so in 2014 when this graph was published in 2017. As you examine the graph, ask yourself, does the graph support diversity among professors at our universities, or does it support the belief that students are being indoctrinated to accept the theories of Socialism, Marxism, DEI, etc.?

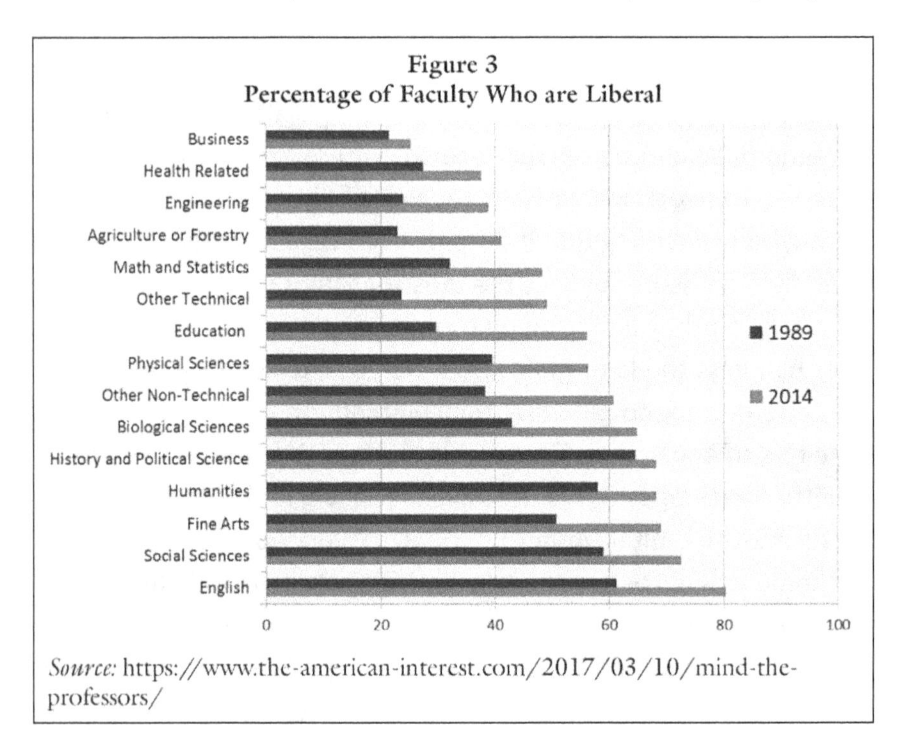

While writing this book, I learned about a four-day seminar for the American School Counselors Association (ASCA) held in Austin, Texas, in July 2022. The seminar was entitled "No Limits." Before I offer excerpts from the conference, let me provide some context to the ASCA. Before 2014, this association was politically neutral and did not interfere in a student's personal life.

Since 2012, the ASCA has been guilty of pushing the association's ideology onto students, teachers, school counselors, and parents (if they can succeed with this population as well). For example, in 2021, their position statement was as follows, "It is an expectation, not the exception" for school counselors to integrate multiculturalism and social justice into their work as advocate leaders. Furthermore, their goals are to stand up against what they believe to be anti-racism and anti-parental rights and favor diversity, equity, inclusion, and Critical Race Theory.

Diversity and Critical Race Theory will be presented in Chapter 8, but I want to address equity and inclusion here. So, let's tackle "inclusion" first. In the publication from Very Well Mind, they defined inclusion as "the act or practice of including and accommodating people who have historically been excluded because of their race, gender, sexuality, or ability." As a goal, this is fine; so long as we achieve inclusion, by making sure others are not left out. An example would be affirmative action, as it appears in the university setting where certain minority groups are given preference in their admission while other races or cultures are not. So, inclusion is okay if it does not lead to reverse discrimination. The goal is to ensure everyone is included and no one is excluded because of race, gender, etc.

So, now, let's discuss equality vs. equity. In today's discussion, some believe, including the ASCA, that before equality can be achieved, there must first be equity. So, how are the two defined? The following quotes from GW Online Public Health from November 5, 2020, entitled, "Equity vs. Equality, What's The Difference?" "Equality means each individual or group of people is given the same resources or opportunities. Equity recognizes that each person has different circumstances and allocates the exact resources and opportunities needed to reach an equal outcome." So, in this context, the folks pushing for equity are looking to achieve a specific, what they refer to as "an equal outcome" for everyone. However, equity is not about equal opportunity for all. Equity equals discrimination. For equity to occur, someone has to be deprived so someone else can be chosen as the winner. Equity is not about choosing or even considering who is the most qualified.

Regarding equality and equity, Aristotle said the challenge of Democracy is when a man votes equally for another person, then he may feel logically that the government must make him equal in every other aspect, which entails a loss of liberty and freedom. Alexis De Tocqueville was worried that the problem in America would be that the majority of the people would rather all be poorer and equal than some being better off from others and being more equal than others.

Choosing equity over equality would mean folks are not selected because they are the most qualified but to fulfill some type of quota. In the real world, an example would be an individual who is chosen to be a pilot or a doctor, not because of their aptitude but because other factors (such as race or gender) are considered over the best qualified. When boarding a plane or are scheduled for surgery, we want to be confident that the pilot flying the plane is most competent to get us to our destination or that the surgeon is successful in the operating room and helping the patient to recuperate from the procedure. The problem with affirmative action or quotas is that the public will wonder if an individual or individuals who were hired or promoted through affirmative action or quotas were the most qualified or whether the person or committee was just checking the equity box in filling the job with a particular minority.

Let me offer my own example. In professional tennis, whether it is with men or women, there are height and talent disparities. Tennis players of all nationalities compete not only in the four Grand Slams (the US Open, the French Open, the Australian, and Wimbledon) but in other tournaments throughout the year. Yet, each individual who strives to be a professional and ultimately wins tournaments, every player is expected to make decisions about how committed they will be to be their best. One can make the same comparison with basketball, where players compete at differing heights. It isn't about race or culture. Each player knows the rules of their sport and uses their talent to achieve their goal. In each sport, it shouldn't be about equity to achieve a particular outcome. That would Include those who were born men and transition and then call themselves females should not be allowed to compete in women's sports, whether it is tennis or swimming or any other competition.

So, back to the ASCA conference that occurred in July 2022, the Ethics Chairman and past president of this association, Carolyn Stone, said, "Our kids are being erased by laws such as the Parents Bill of Rights, the Stop Woke Act. There's actually a Stop Woke Act. You refuse to remain comfortable in your own role as long as there's one student left out of the success equation. Yes, learn the rules so you know how to break them."

During the conference, Ms. Stone did not believe parents should have any rights while they are in the custody of public schools. As I was viewing her comments during the conference, there was a poster of the US. In the upper right-hand corner was the word "Transgender," and in the lower left-hand corner was the word "Abortion," and at the bottom of the poster was the following caption, "It Matters Where You Live: Community and Institutional Standards." And here is Ms. Stone's quote, with this poster visible, "One of the things we have to always factor in, as educators, is the fact that we are in a setting where parents are made to relinquish custody and control of their children. Now think about that. There is no other setting or time when a parent is made to give control of their child. We also have to factor in the fact in where you live, folks. It does, doesn't it? It matters that there are two school counselors right now in Florida who have had lawsuits filed against them because they did not alert parents when the child told them (the school counselors) about their need to transition. So, it matters where you are. Some states you're not in, you won't have to be dealing with those issues quite the way the rest of us are. So, it's not ethics that are a one-size-fits-all, as you know. Ethics are situational. You have to apply them where you live. I can't behave in Florida the way a New York City counselor can behave."

There is so much to unpack from Ms. Stone's comments and the views of this association. Ethics and parental rights were mentioned. Parents should not relinquish their rights when their child enters the school building. It is still their child to raise. The only responsibility the school should have is to educate each child and not to inject their liberal philosophies, such as their interpretation of social justice.

Regarding ethics, from the example of children wanting to transition, the school and school counselors should not ethically be involved in children wishing to transition and whether or not parents are notified. It is my belief that no child should be allowed to transition until they reach the age of adulthood. The ASCA and all other mental health professional organizations and associations should refrain from taking political stands. And the ethics they adopt should be consistent across all 50 states.

Let me return to the subject of our children and adolescents' education. Rather than allowing our children and adolescents to be brainwashed and indoctrinated, I propose that we teach them to be critical thinkers. There are many examples where teachers and professors present theories. Then they attempt to tell students that their view or theory is a proven fact and based on science. And they may state that "a consensus of scientists have concluded..." but a consensus of scientists is not science. Once upon a time, a consensus of scientists believed the world was flat.

Here is an example of our own profession. Many years ago, it was once thought that children and adolescents would outgrow their diagnosis of ADD (Attention Deficit Disorder) or ADHD (Attention Deficit Disorder With Hyperactivity). We now know that children and teens still have the same symptoms, but they often compensate as they get older. So, just because the so-called experts in our field believed something and had it accepted for so many years does not make it a fact. Their conclusions were proven to have been erroneous.

I believe in keeping America as an exceptional country as it has been in the past. Our country has always been the first in innovative entrepreneurs, showing the rest of the world what freedom and self-determination look like and being the world's envy. That would include us as clinicians, as we have chosen this profession to help others and perhaps those who wish to start their own private practice as a business. These concepts begin with the education of our children and making sure that all of their endeavors and goals are desirable and accomplishable.

Everything I have raised in this chapter is vital because I want our youth to strive to be the best they can be. I do not want them to accept anything presented to them out of dogma. So, to support these goals, whether in counseling or in our society, including parents, educators, therapists, and everyone else our youth encounters, I want to be motivated to succeed educationally, vocationally, and in life.

So, let me end this chapter on a positive note. I have the following posted on my bulletin board in my private practice office. It is entitled "150 Ways To Show (Your) Kids You Care," written by Jolene L. Roehikepartain in 2005 by Search Institute. I will not share all 150 suggestions but will highlight the ones I believe are important. "Notice them, acknowledge them, seek them out, listen to them, give them eye contact, play with them, read aloud together, tell them their feelings are okay, set boundaries that keep them safe, be honest, be yourself, listen to their stories, hug them and tell them you love them a lot, forget your worries as often as you can so you concentrate on them, notice when they are acting differently, present options when they seek your counsel, surprise them and hide surprises for them to find, stay with them when they are afraid. Suggest better behaviors when they act out, show delight in their discoveries, laugh at their jokes, kneel or squat or sit so that you are at their eye level, answer their questions, tell them how terrific they are, use your ears more than your mouth, make yourself available, find common interests, listen to their music, hold hands during walks, thank them and praise them for any behavior you want them to repeat, seek and encourage win-win solutions, give them your undivided attention, ask for their opinion, have fun together, meet their friends, allow them to solve their own problems, let them tell you how they feel, praise more than you admonish, be consistent, admit when you make a mistake, ask them to help you, support them and applaud their successes, believe in them, allow them to make mistakes, respect them, appreciate their individuality, accept them for who they are, become their advocate, trust them, help them to make good decisions and choices, expect their best but don't expect perfection, cook and share a meal together and finally, love them no matter what." If parents will apply these suggestions, not only can they be proud of their efforts, but they will have helped their children to be their best and to succeed in all their endeavors.

CHAPTER 4:

Violence In The US And Sensible Remedies

WHEN I WAS writing this book, a school shooting occurred at Robb Elementary School in Uvalde, Texas, where a male shot and killed young children and two teachers. I had not considered a chapter on school shootings or violence in the US until I learned about the shooter's psychological makeup. In this chapter, I also want to focus on the various methods of violence against their victims, the possible causes, and various solutions to consider to stem this violence.

Look at the recent headlines across the country, and you will find the following: a driver plows their car into a crowd, killing and injuring many pediatricians; an individual throws his victim in front of a subway car; an assailant stabs his victim to death, bombings such as the one that occurred at the Boston Marathon. Of course, there are multiple instances where guns have been used as an instrument for inflicting death on their victims.

I want to focus on the psychological makeup of the assailants and their similarities. So, let's look at the psychological makeup of the adolescent of the Robb Elementary School shooting (I will not refer to him by name) who was responsible for the multiple deaths.

There were instances where he cut on his face just for the fun of his actions; he was made fun of and bullied for stuttering; he dropped out of school, was estranged from his mother, and went to live with his grandmother. The red flags continued. Before the shooting, he had just purchased a fully automatic rifle and hundreds of rounds. He posted on Facebook that he was going to shoot his grandmother and again posted that he had done so and that he would shoot up an elementary school and shoot as many individuals as he could. His mother was interviewed, and even though she said she could not believe her son had inflicted the carnage, she did reveal that he was a loner with few friends. He tended to gravitate towards violent gaming sites. She appeared to defend her son by saying he was not violent but could be quite aggressive when he was angry. She also stated about her son, "We all have a rage, and some have it more than others." That quote came from an ABC News report by Matt Gutman et al. entitled "Mother of Texas Gunman Says Son Was 'Not A Monster' Could Be 'Aggressive.' on May 26, 2022. Unfortunately, none of these warning signs were picked up by law enforcement or his mother or grandparents. Perhaps because he dropped out of school, he was never seen by a school counselor or resource officer.

Unfortunately, there have been too many school shootings. As I share details about these school shootings, again, I will not identify the shooters by name but will share other pertinent information such as where they occurred, information on the shooting, and the shooter's motivations and psychological makeup. The FBI defines a mass shooting as killing four or more people, not including the shooter or shooters.

In 1764, the first mass shooting occurred when three men entered a schoolhouse near present-day Greencastle, Pennsylvania, and reportedly killed ten people. It wasn't until 1966 that the next mass shooting occurred when a 25-year-old man went on a 96-minute shooting spree from an observation deck at the University of Texas. He had also murdered his wife and mother earlier that day before arriving at the university. This shooter, for my purposes, does not fit the profile because it is suspected that the cause of his actions was a brain tumor, not because of psychological issues.

In the first mass school shooting, the public and the media agree that the first one happened at Columbine in 1999, and here are some details about the two shooters. They wrote hate stories and letters that were perceived as having a potential for violence. In addition, they wrote a paper on school shootings and completed a research paper on Charles Manson and the Nazis.

The next mass school shooting happened at Virginia Tech in 2007. The shooter had a long list of mental health problems dating back to his early childhood. He was diagnosed with severe depression and severe social anxiety disorder. His troubling incidents led him to receive therapy at the university counseling center. Other incidents came to the attention of the campus police and the dean of student affairs, but none of these incidents were shared due to privacy laws.

In 2012, at Sandy Hook Elementary in Newtown, Connecticut, the assailant had a history of social, emotional, and developmental issues. In the 5th grade, he wrote a comic book filled with violent drawings. He also wrote stories of child murder and cannibalism. In the 7th grade, he constructed stories about battles, war, and destruction. He had feelings of rage, hate, and homicidal impulses. His mother took him out of school and home-schooled him. Before the school shooting, he shot and killed his mother in the home where he lived.

The next mass school shooting I want to include occurred at Marjory Stoneman Douglas High School in Parkland, FL, in 2018. At the age of 13, this eventual shooter received 26 disciplinary incidents in one year. He was suspended for fighting and was transferred to a school with fellow students with similar emotional and behavioral problems. He had told an administrator that shooting guns helped to relieve his stress. It was determined later that he met the criteria for aggression and depression and had a fascination with guns. However, his behavior was never shared with authority officials, which could have resulted in his getting help for his psychological care.

Again, while writing this book, another shooting occurred in Highland Park, IL, known as the 4th of July shooting. Here are the facts that were brought out after the shooting. In April 2019, when the eventual shooter was 19, he attempted suicide. In September 2019.

the police were called to his parent's residence after this individual threatened to kill everyone in the home. The police confiscated several knives, a sword, and a dagger. The parents decided not to pursue a formal complaint against their son, so this incident wasn't noted in their son's record. In Illinois, a minor wishing to purchase a firearm must have a parent or guardian to sponsor the applicant and sign an affidavit stating that the sponsor, who is allowing the purchase, will be held liable for any damages resulting from the minor's use of the firearm. In December 2019, when the individual was 19 years old, his father sponsored an application allowing his son to purchase a rifle. Finally, in June 2020, he passed four background checks when purchasing additional firearms. This individual had posted two music videos depicting some kind of shooting and shared a photo of a politician who killed himself during a live press conference. He posted thousands and shared violent images and videos of people dying.

Here is some additional information about the 4th of July shooter from The New York Post: Opinion from writer Miranda Devine, entitled "Did reefer drive the Highland Park parade killer... to madness?" (July 6, 2022). The shooter was described as timid and quiet. The family could be labeled as dysfunctional as there was a lot of yelling at each other. After the son was arrested, his mother screamed "at the police outside her home and exposing her breast at them." She further wrote, "In 2015, when he was 14, his mother was reportedly charged with domestic battery over "a physical dispute that had occurred while driving" at 3:37 a.m. near the family home, in the affluent Chicago suburb of Highland Park, according to a police report posted on the website Patch. Another witness said, "it seemed like her kids were a nuisance to her." His parents were separated, and the son lived with his father and uncle at the time of the shooting.

So, what are the characteristics that most schools and mass shooters have in common? They tend to be Caucasian males who are isolated and/or rejected and bullied by their peers. Regardless of whether peers bullied them, they might have kept a list of perceived grievances Inflicted upon them. Some were fascinated by predecessors, so they planned their violent acts as a way to copycat and/or for their own notoriety. They may be disruptive in their school behavior. They tend to come from troubled homes and often live in a rural community. And they have easy access to weapons. Finally, some were fascinated with gaming sites, violent video games, comics, and movies that glorified violence.

In Chapter 7, I will discuss the use of medications that might be needed to treat these types of clients and, hopefully, that may help us achieve counseling goals more successfully. However, I want to include an article in this discussion that makes a villain out of the medications that shooters took at the time of their killing spree. The name of the article is "Every Mass Shooting Shares One Thing In Common & It's Not Weapons" (https://www.ammoland.com/2013/04/every-mass-shooting-in-the-last-20-years-shares-psychotropic-drugs/#ixzz7Y1X-LtbCQ). The article accuses Selective Serotonin Re-Uptake Inhibitors (SSRIs) that these shooters were taking as the cause or at least a contributing factor. The author made a list of mass shooters and the psychotropic drugs they were prescribed from 1999 until the article was written in 2013.

Before I continue to discuss the article, let's define what an SSRI is along with psychotropic medications. The following came from Shodair Children's Hospital and the article "Psychotropic Medications For Children." "Psychotropic medications act on the brain and central nervous system. They change the way chemicals in the brain called "neurotransmitters" send messages between brain cells through a synapse or crossing. Each psychotropic medication is used to treat certain "target" symptoms." They can target symptoms of attention deficit disorder (ADD), conduct disorder, oppositional defiant disorder, anxiety, depression, bipolar, obsessive-compulsive disorder (OCD), and post-traumatic stress disorder (PTSD). The classes of psychotropic medications are stimulants, antidepressants, antipsychotics, mood stabilizers, and anxiolytics.

There are several problems with this article "Every Mass Shooting Shares One Thing In Common & It's Not Weapons" conclusions. I want to include a rebuttal from the author of "The Musings of a Christian Psychologist entitled, "Do Psychotropic Drugs Cause Violence and Aggression?" Phillip Monroe, June 20, 2015, stated, "There is little evidence that SSRIs and other psychotropic medications can cause or even encourage violence. What is true is that violence, like everything else, is a multifactored event. Those prone to addiction, isolation, delusion, paranoia, impulse control problems may have increased risk to resort to violence."

Continuing with my issues with the article, "Every Mass Shooting Shares One Thing In Common & It's Not Weapons," the author fails to note why these shooters were prescribed their medications in the first place. These shooters appeared to be exhibiting symptoms that warranted the prescription that was subsequently prescribed. There is ample evidence that psychotropic medications have been effective in treating the symptoms for which they were prescribed. In this chapter, the focus will not be on the medications but instead on the psychological makeup of the individual who ultimately took the lives of others. Again, in Chapter 7, I will continue this discussion on medications.

Now that we have a list of the common characteristics these adolescents and young adults shared and where the shootings took place, I think it is a legitimate question to ask: what has been driving all of this since the Columbine shooting happened in 1999?

Is it because, for many families, both parents have to work, whereas, in previous generations, the mother could stay home and raise the children? Is it because, in many cases, the divorce rate has continued to increase, single parents are raising children and adolescents, and sometimes the father is absent altogether from the family? Is it because parents have not taught their children about morals, right and wrong, and the family belonging to some type of religion? Finally, is it partly due to parents not knowing what their children are viewing on social media and allowing their male children to become perhaps addicted to violent gaming sites? There are probably more questions to ask, and similar ones have had an impact on adults.

John Iannarelli, in his book, "How To Spot A Terrorist Before It Is Too Late," stated that it starts with the parents noticing changes in their children's behavior, attitude, and a decline in their school grades; if they have been fired from their job or they cannot keep a job. Other indicators include irritability and symptoms of anxiety or depression. If they are taking medications, are they taking them as prescribed? Many of these sufferers go undiagnosed. Some individuals have a history of being physically, emotionally, and/or sexually abused, neglected, or bullied. Many have repeatedly been exposed to traumatic incidents. He further asserts that parents, teachers, and neighbors need to report their observations of a mood disorder, psychotic, or anxiety to authorities so that action can be taken to prevent a potential shooting.

It also seems that, as a society, human life is not viewed as precious as it once was in previous generations. One can continue to vilify guns, but one can also argue that guns have always been around. The difference seems to be how easy it is to take a life, whether by gun, car, knife or by our hands. However, it seems reasonable to support what is referred to as "red flag laws." Red flag laws would allow family members, police officers, and school officials to file for an extreme risk protection order in court in some states. One's firearms would be confiscated, requiring a judge to grant a hearing to determine if an individual is a danger to himself or others. In that case, typically, a hearing must be held within two weeks to determine if the person should be restricted from accessing firearms for an extended time. I would favor individual states establishing their own red flag laws rather than trusting the federal government to implement one for the entire country. It would also allow an individual to press charges against a family member or neighbor who has filed a false extreme risk protection order out of spite, revenge, or anger, and the individual posed no risk.

Some oppose red flag laws because the opponents state that an individual must have a due process hearing before their firearms are confiscated. But suppose the law is applied consistently, and an individual is suspected to be in danger of harming themselves or others. In that case, the individual can be picked up by law enforcement and taken to a psychiatric facility for about three days. Then, a hearing is held, and a judge determines if the individual poses that risk. If the individual does pose such a risk, the judge would require the individual to remain in the facility. However, the judge can rule that the individual receives psychiatric services outside of a hospital. So, already, there are laws and precedence in place when an individual is suspected that they may harm either themselves or others. In this instance, it makes sense to require that one's firearms be taken away until the hearing determines that the individual poses no risk. To the contrary, If the individual does pose such a risk and is allowed to keep their guns knowing that the hearing has been scheduled, they may use that firearm to take their life or others.

If the goal is putting reasonable solutions in place that may reduce gun violence, then red-flag laws and filing an extreme risk protection order in court may be one such remedy. On the other hand, if it is abused and family members, spouses, ex-spouses, or neighbors file false affidavits, there should be harsh penalties for their vengeful actions. However, if the risk protection order is filed with no malice because it was suspected that an individual posed a risk, and a hearing showed that risk was prevalent. In this scenario, the firearms would have been confiscated, which would have prevented a violent act. Now, does it make sense to support such a law?

With the increase in school shootings, the debate on guns focuses on what our politicians should do to address these tragedies and what the populace will accept. As this book is being written, one suggestion is not allowing eighteen-year-olds to purchase a rifle until they are 21. Why does this make sense? If the logic applies that they are not mature enough to own a rifle or a handgun, then does the same reasoning apply to this logic: they are not mature enough to join the military or vote until they are 21? Of course, our society and politicians would disagree with this logic. So, let's break it down. In the military, 18-year-olds are trained to use the weapon they will be carrying. Well, that makes sense. We require drivers to pass a test before they are given a license. Common sense dictates that perhaps we should consider requiring firearms training on how to use the weapon the individual (all adult individuals) will be purchasing.

Some options would make schools safer, and I believe these recommendations are commonsensical. First, encourage schools to have a zero-tolerance for threats made by students. In several school shootings, school administrators received evidence of danger from teachers, students, and even the individuals who made the threats. Next, implement security procedures by teaching staff and students about the need for lockdowns when a threat has been received. Students' backpacks and lockers will be inspected if a threat is suspected. Another suggestion is to add security and hardware at every school. There is hardware that can strengthen school door locks that school administrators can research to determine if they are needed. These would include adding and using metal detectors whenever anyone enters the building. Also, parents must check in at the school reception area every time they enter the building. There should be only one door when students and staff enter the buildings. No entry or exit doors should ever be propped open or even unlocked. Banks have security guards; there should be no reason schools are not provided with the same security. If armed security handles the entrance door, they would be responsible for opening it for students and staff. They would be responsible for ensuring that the entrance door cannot be opened from the outside. Supposedly, this is how the Uvalde shooter entered the school because one of the entrance doors was not secure. Finally, there ought to be no tolerance for bullying. Frequently, children do not believe they will be listened to or feel protected when they report these incidents to administrators.

So far, the focus has been on the psychological makeup of the typical school shooter. Now, let's include the adult mass murderer.

Although many of the characteristics of the mass murderer are similar to those of the school shooter, there is also a common denominator between mass murderers and school shooters. Many of these individuals heavily used marijuana at a young age.

There was the individual who shot and killed many at a Texas church in November 2017, and it was revealed that he had marijuana in his system. A week after the killings in Texas, a California "pot farmer" murdered several and injured many others. A Japanese man who stabbed and killed many disabled people in 2016 frequently advocated for marijuana legalization. Just weeks before his attack, he had been diagnosed with cannabis-induced psychosis and paranoia. Heavy or very heavy use of marijuana at a young age that includes the Planned Parenthood shooter, the Aurora shooter, the Tucson shooter, and the Chattanooga shooter. The Chattanooga shooter suffered mainly from depression and/or bipolar disorder. He was a heavy marijuana user, which was an essential part of his life and prevented him from getting a job. The Colorado Springs shooter had become an early pot addict and tried to recover. When he began using marijuana again after Colorado legalized it, he immediately became psychotic. Before the shooting, he had been trying to seek mental health treatment. His toxicology report tested THC+, and no other drugs were found in his system. The Oklahoma bomber and the Boston Marathon bombers were also regular marijuana users.

In 2014, in Washington State, a high school student shot five friends he had invited to eat lunch with him. Then, on Twitter, he revealed the need to smoke a lot of pot because of a breakup with his girlfriend, who said she had broken up with him because smoking pot made him stupid. He was only 15 then, but Washington State started selling commercialized pot about four months earlier.

Referring back to the 4th of July shooter, he also habitually smoked cannabis. Again, from the New York Post Opinion from writer Miranda Devine, entitled "Did reefer drive the Highland Park parade killer to madness?" (July 6, 2022), a former friend of the shooter said he was "an isolated stoner who completely lost touch with reality."

The editor and author of the publication "Parents Opposed To Pot: Bursting The Bubble of Marijuana Hype" wrote the article, "Marijuana Is The Common Web Between So Many Mass Killers, July 3, 2018, and he stated, "The 15% or so of marijuana users who experience psychotic symptoms from marijuana or go into permanent psychosis (schizophrenia) are 9x more likely to become violent than schizophrenics whose illness has nothing to do with drugs."

In March 2020, the National Institute of Health article "A Review of Cases of Pot and Violence" found that "recent illicit and medical pot is much more potent and more likely to cause violent behavior and is a predictable and preventable cause of tragic, violent consequences."

The findings mentioned above were supported in the New York Post article by Miranda Devine which stated, "The Link Between Pot And Mass Shootings May Be Closer Than We Think." The report stated, "A seminal long-term study of 50,465 Swedish army conscripts found those who had tried marijuana by age 18 had 2.4 times the risk of being diagnosed with schizophrenia in the following 15 years than those who had never used the drug. Heavy users were 6.7 times more likely to be admitted to a hospital for schizophrenia." In states where marijuana has become legalized, hospital emergency rooms have seen a daily occurrence of adolescents seeking treatment for cannabis-induced psychosis.

In previous generations, the THC potency was around 3%, whereas now, the potency is about 17%. In a Mayo Clinic article from September 26, 2018, entitled "How Teen Marijuana Use Impacts Brain Development." The author, Dr. Pravesh Sharma, a psychiatrist from Esau Claire, Wisconsin, noted a survey that found that, although marijuana use is prevalent among adolescents and young adults, they are in doubt that it can cause harm. Dr. Sharma stated that their perceived beliefs that marijuana use poses little risk could lead to future increased use. Dr. Sharma continued, "The adolescent or teen brain continues to mature and develop until around age 25, especially in areas of the brain involved in planning, decision-making, and learning, which develops last. This time window is considered a window of vulnerability where any disruption has abnormal and unwanted consequences. This causes learning, memory, coordination, reaction time, and judgment problems. It also can cause hallucinations, paranoia, and a range of emotional problems. Marijuana use may lead to academic difficulties, poor sports performance, impaired driving, and troubled relationships."

Dr. Sharma concludes by stating, "Not every teen or young adult who uses marijuana becomes addicted because every person reacts differently. The effects of marijuana on an individual depends on the concentration of THC in the marijuana product used, family history of addiction, and person's genetic susceptibility to addiction, addiction to other drugs and alcohol, environment and history of psychiatric illness. Those who start using marijuana at an early age, in high amounts and with risk factors mentioned above, are more prone to developing marijuana use disorder."

One more study needs to be included because it is the most recent when this book was written. The study is entitled "New Study: Marijuana Users Three Times More Likely To Develop Peripheral Artery Disease." The study was presented at the Society for Cardiovascular Angiography & Interventions (SCAI) 2023 Scientific Sessions and highlights the connection between marijuana use and peripheral artery disease (PAD). The study's results suggested that marijuana users are significantly more likely to develop PAD compared to those in the broader population." The author continued, "While many studies have looked at the impact of marijuana use on health, little research has been done to study the effect of marijuana use on the vascular system. PAD, a condition in which narrowed arteries reduce blood flow to the arms or legs, impacts 6.5 million people in the U.S. and can lead to a loss of mobility, reduced quality of life, heart attack, stroke, and death if not treated early.

Out of the 30 million patients identified in the study, 623,768 were diagnosed as marijuana users. Patients with an average age of 37.4 years and equal distribution across genders were more likely to be white and more likely to be elective admissions. Out of all these patients, 2,424 (0.38%) were also diagnosed with PAD. Hirva Vyas, D.O., Hackensack University Medical Center, Hackensack, NJ, and lead author of the study, said, "Symptoms of PAD such as leg pain while walking, slower or no hair growth, and feelings of coldness in the leg. We know PAD is a progressive disease that can drastically impact the quality of life, making ongoing monitoring of this patient population critical."

Therefore, it does not make any sense for states to have bowed to the whims of the public in legalizing marijuana without having public hearings on what effect (mentally, psychologically, and medically) this drug will have on adolescents and adults. Also, in states where marijuana has been legalized, driving under the influence (DUI) and traffic accidents and fatalities have increased.

Here is data supporting the evidence that DUIs, traffic injuries, and fatalities have increased, and that data comes from the Insurance Institute For Highway Safety (IIHS). "The Insurance Institute for Highway Safety (IIHS) is an independent, nonprofit scientific and educational organization dedicated to reducing deaths, injuries and property damage from motor vehicle crashes through research, evaluation, and through education of consumers, policymakers and safety professionals." Their article entitled, "Crash Rates Jump in Wake of Marijuana Legalization, New Study Shows," reported that, "Crash rates spiked with the legalization of recreational marijuana use and retail sales in California, Colorado, Nevada, Oregon, and Washington, a new study by the Insurance Institute for Highway Safety (IIHS) and another by the affiliated Highway Loss Data Institute (HLDI) show."

The IIHS report continued, "Consumption also appears to be expanding rapidly, with self-reports of past-month marijuana use doubling from 6 percent to 12 percent of those surveyed between 2008 and 2019. That's a potential concern for those who care about road safety. Driving simulator tests have shown that drivers who are high on marijuana react more slowly, find it harder to pay attention, have more difficulty maintaining their car's position in the lane, and make more errors when something goes wrong than when they're sober. But such tests have also shown that marijuana-impaired drivers are likely to drive at slower speeds, make fewer attempts to overtake, and keep more distance between their vehicle and the one ahead of them. The most recent of these studies from IIHS shows that injury and fatal crash rates in California, Colorado, Nevada, Oregon, and Washington jumped in the months following the relaxation of marijuana laws in each state. "All this so that these states can profit from the sale of legalized pot!"

I want to focus on our responsibilities for the rest of this chapter. I believe that we should make the parents accountable, not after a tragedy, but be proactive before it even happens. And in 2024, a court agreed with this assertion. On November 30, 2021, at Oxford High School in Oxford, Michigan, a student shot and killed four classmates and wounded seven others. On April 9. 2024, Fox 4 News in Dallas reported that the parents were tried and convicted of involuntary manslaughter for their gross negligence after they ignored their son's warning signs before the shooting. Instead, they purchased a handgun for their son just four days before the shooting. Seven months prior to his shooting rampage, he had texted a friend, "I actually asked my dad to take me to the doctor yesterday but he just gave me pills and told me to 'Suck it up.'" In the same text message, he said he asked his mom to take him to the doctor, and she laughed at him.

Some legal experts believe the conviction of these parents will set a dangerous precedence. It seems, without a doubt, that this adolescent's warning signs were ignored by his parents, and thus, the parents should face the consequences of their son's actions. I believe there should be Public Service Announcements (PSAs) on TV to educate parents, grandparents, and school officials on behaviors to be acquainted with and how to bring them to the attention of those who can intervene. Past PSAs have been used to educate adults and adolescents about the hazards of alcohol and drug use. There was an effective one called the "Crying Indian," whose PSA message was Keep America Beautiful. Each of them has been effective.

Another responsibility is to adequately assess the individual who comes to our office and possesses the psychological characteristics of a potential shooter. For example, for those of us who see adolescents, our clients might be brought in by parents or referred to us by their school. So, let's discuss what goes into those psychological assessments. Let's start with the assessments that are often used with children and adolescents first. There are many to choose from, but you want to use ones that answer the following questions: the child/adolescent's mental status, their thought process and verbalizations, their dreams, drawings, wishes, their concept of themselves, their ability to make and maintain friends, if they have siblings, the birth order, how they get along with their siblings, how they deal with anger and frustration, do they prefer to be with others or being alone, their relationships with teachers and classmates and many other questions too numerous to list.

Other suggestions are to carefully examine your child/adolescent client and assess whether they look happy or unhappy, depressed or elated, calm or jittery, clumsy or well-coordinated. I usually ask questions about things such as their interest in sports. If they are interested, which sport do they prefer to watch or participate? You could ask if learning to be good at a sport came naturally or required much effort. You can ask the same questions about school and grades. Which subjects are their favorite and why, and which are challenging and why? Do they like school, and regarding grades, are their grades vital to them, or do they do just enough to pass their subjects? These questions are designed to establish a rapport and gleam with the individual you are assessing.

You also want to ask if the family has had pets and how the child/adolescent treated the pet(s). Again, you always want to establish a rapport with every client as you weave the questions you want to pose. Gather as much information as possible from parents, including those asked about their child and the child's medical history (including the mother's pregnancy and anything remarkable about the birth). Are the parents still married or divorced? If parents are divorced, how old was the child when the divorce occurred, how did the child react, and was school/grades impacted? How is the child or adolescent's relationship with each parent?

Also, obtain information from the school where the child or adolescent attends and have the school include any scholastic tests given. If possible, seek past school records from previous schools as well. Finally, if you are in private practice or a clinical setting where you are employed, I believe it is essential to have established professional relationships with psychiatrists. In addition to the psychological assessment you are conducting, it would be vital to have a psychiatrist evaluate them and provide feedback to you, the clinician.

Everything mentioned about the need to evaluate children and adolescents that you suspect are imminently at risk of harming themselves or others also holds true for adults who come through our counseling door. As stated earlier in this chapter, there has been a rise in violence in our country, so it is essential to assess for imminent risk. It is just as vital that we emphasize in the Statement of Understanding that we have the clients sign before counseling is initiated and that we will break confidentiality if there is an imminent risk of either the client harming themselves or someone else.

There has also been an increase in the need to help clients with anger management and teach them appropriate coping skills as they are dealing with emotions such as frustration and agitation to more extreme emotions such as rage. Even we, as clinicians who practice in large cities, may have to deal with clients who, for instance, admit to road rage incidents.

While I was counseling a male client, the Uvalde shooting occurred. The client wanted to take a few of his sessions to process the events that happened on the day of the shooting. He said he was a proponent of gun control in his stance to make schools safer and prevent future school shootings. In earlier chapters, I emphasized how important it is to avoid verbal arguments with clients. In this case, I believed it would be advantageous to the client to help him process his feelings, and I allowed him to share his views on guns. Although, in the discussion, he disclosed that an invention could strengthen school locks. I supported his assertion that this would be something to advocate in our schools. At the end of this discussion on strategies that would make schools safer, it was essential to find solutions that the client found acceptable. Because we always want to assist them in accomplishing their therapeutic goals and not get bogged down in trying to convince one another on controversial issues such as gun control. I learned a long time ago such discussions on controversial topics such as gun control, the right to choose abortion over the right to life, and politics have no place in the therapeutic setting.

Chapter 5:

Current (Perhaps Permanent) Conditions Affecting The Mental Health of Children, Adolescents & Adults

The Wuhan Virus (COVID-19)

I CHOSE TO call it The Wuhan Virus because the virus originated at a lab in Wuhan China. I decided not to be politically correct by referring to it as COVID-19 or the coronavirus. In February 2023, both the US Energy Dept and the Director of the FBI finally admitted that the Wuhan virus originated at the Laboratory of Virology. There is precedence in naming viruses from the area where they originated. For example, MERS-CoV is the Middle East Respiratory Syndrome Coronavirus, a viral respiratory illness first reported in Saudi Arabia in 2012. And, of course, you have heard of the West Nile virus, which originated in Uganda. Referring to this virus as the Wuhan virus does not make one xenophobic. According to the Oxford Learner's Dictionary, xenophobia is defined as "having or showing a dislike or prejudice against people from other countries." It just indicates consistency in giving it the name where it was discovered.

How has this virus impacted our lives, from adults to children and adolescents? It led government officials to issue stay-at-home orders, travel bans, restrictions on meeting with family members, friends, and neighbors, and the closure of non-essential stores, gyms, movie theatres, museums, art galleries, and even places of worship.

On the other hand, some of my clients reported feeling more content because they did not have to face a stressful workplace on a daily basis. Although while working from home, on the one hand, eliminated the stress of the drive time to and from work, many experienced feelings of isolation. They felt cut off from their colleagues and received less social support.

The pandemic also contributed to some employees losing their jobs, and many businesses temporarily or permanently closed their doors. In addition, many expressed feeling depressed and anxious and admitted to having problems falling and staying asleep, with many reporting that they only got about 4 hours of sleep at night. This led many to request anti-depressants, anti-anxiety, and sleep aids from their physician.

I first want to focus on how the shutdowns and school closings due to the Wuhan virus have impacted our children and adolescents. The following article identified the struggles of high school teenagers. The report came from the Medical News Today on March 12, 2021, entitled "Global Impact of the COVID-19 Pandemic: 1 Year On", by Maria Cohut, Ph.D. A 2020 Centers for Disease Control and Prevention. The study found that 1 in 3 high school students and half of the female students reported persistent feelings of sadness and loneliness. This was an increase of 40 percent from 2009 to 2019. These feelings were reinforced by social media blitzing teens with messages telling them they were not good-looking, popular, or intelligent.

We are now discovering the harm done to our children by keeping them out of school because of the Wuhan virus. Once they were allowed to return to school, they were required to wear masks. In the CNN Health article from August 11, 2021, entitled "Does mask wearing harm your child's development? Experts Weigh In," the author, Kristen Rogers, wrote, "For young children, the pandemic comes at a crucial time for developing skills important for empathy, safety and more — a phase that some parents worry will be impaired by mask-wearing." She quoted Ashley Ruba, a postdoctoral researcher in the University of

Wisconsin-Madison's Child Emotion Lab, "There are sensitive periods in early childhood development in which language development and emotional development are really rapidly developing for the first few years of life. Being able to use others' verbal or facial cues to figure out how someone is feeling or pick up on safe or dangerous aspects of environments and people is a critical task for young kids,"

Ruba and her co-author "showed more than 80 children ages 7 to 13 photos of faces that were unobstructed, covered by a surgical mask, or wearing sunglasses. The faces displayed sadness, anger, or fear. When asked to assign one of six emotions to each face, the children were correct about uncovered faces 66% of the time. However, when faces were covered by masks, the children had trouble correctly identifying sadness roughly 28% of the time, anger 27%, and fear 18%, which was more than the odds (about 17%) of correctly guessing one emotion from the six labels." Another expert who was interviewed in this article was Amy Learmonth, a professor of psychology at William Paterson University in New Jersey. She stated her concern for kids whose lingual or social development is atypical. "Anyone who is just a little behind in language development or a little behind in understanding social cues — what concerns me is that they will fall further behind."

In a New York Post article, "Lockdowns Are Breaking Our Kids And The Damage May Be Permanent," from July 17, 2022, author Bethany Mandel wrote, "According to the Centers for Disease Control and Prevention, children's mental-health-related visits to emergency rooms are up by as much as a third, compared to 2019 figures." She further stated, "In a single week in mid-March 2020, kids' lives were turned upside-down. They lost it all in short order: routine, school, friends, and activities. There is no indication if or when things may return to normal, and they are now spending their days glued to Zoom school, isolated and increasingly besieged by the effects of our pandemic-mitigation efforts." She interviewed J.D. Friedman, a clinical psychologist and partner at Baker Street Behavioral Health in Northern New Jersey, for kids who were already predisposed to mental illnesses like depression, anxiety, or OCD (to name a few). Friedman explained that dealing with the impact of the Wuhan virus "can absolutely tip the scales to full-blown pathology." The author, Mandel, continued, "For the average child, the prognosis for long-term mental-health recovery is optimistic. For now. Kids are resilient, but, again, only up to a point." She said this was predicated on not returning to lockdown and closing schools again.

Then there is this article entitled, "Report: Class of 2022 ACT (American College Testing) Scores Lowest in Decades" by Patrick Camp from the Cullman Times, Alabama, October 18, 2022, at 5:28 pm wrote, "October 18—ACT test scores of the graduating class of 2022 were made public in a report published last week which shows results being the lowest in more than three decades — a result that many officials believe showcase the extent of learning loss brought on by the COVID-19 pandemic."

An internet search will show that due to school closings during the Wuhan Virus, students in virtually every state had a decline in math, reading, and science. I will include just one as an example. The following comes from CNN, entitled, "Nation's Report Card Shows New Evidence of COVID-19 Devastating Impact on US Children's Education," by Ray Sanchez on 10/24/2022. He wrote, "Fourth-and eighth-graders fell behind in reading and had the largest ever decline in math, according to a national educational assessment showing the devastating effect of the Covid-19 pandemic on America's children." Later in the article, he continued, "No state or large urban district showed improvements in math, the report said. Eighth-grade math scores sank in the more than 50 states and jurisdictions participating in the assessment." The decline was a response to the "pandemic in the US, where schools were shut down and teachers turned to online learning."

An article by Michael Lee from Fox News entitled, "Pandemic Learning Loss Could Cost Students Thousands In Income Over Their Lifetime: Study." His article discusses the research of Eric A. Hanushek from Stanford University. Mr. Hanushek's study was entitled "The Economic Cost of the Pandemic," and it "analyzed National Assessment of Educational Progress data and found that between 2019 and 2022, test scores analyzed National Assessment of Educational Progress data and found that between 2019 and 2022, test scores in math and English dropped an average of eight points across the country. "The drastic drop came after nearly two decades of progress, the study noted, erasing all the gains in test scores made between 2000 and 2019." Hanushek stated, " There is overwhelming evidence that students in school during the closure period and during the subsequent adjustments to the pandemic are achieving at significantly lower levels than would have been expected without the pandemic."

The Stanford study went on to predict that "students enrolled in schools during pandemic restrictions will face an average of a two to nine percent drop in lifetime earnings, resulting in states facing a 0.6 to 2.9 percent drop in total GDP" (Gross Domestic Product). In addition, Dr. Hanushek said that unless schools can make strides for the declines, students who were victims of school closures during the pandemic "will enter the workforce with lower cognitive skills needed to succeed in a constantly evolving economy."

Then, there is this article entitled "Study Finds COVID-Related School Closures Increased Mental Health Risks For Young People" from the publication Texas Standard: The National Daily News Show of Texas on July 21, 2022. Jeff Temple, the Vice Dean for research at the University of Texas Medical Branch in Galveston, was interviewed. He and his researchers found that some children who were unable to attend school during COVID lockdowns have missed developmental milestones. He went on to say that while lockdowns early in the pandemic were necessary to prevent the spread of the virus, keeping young people out of schools put an unprecedented mental health strain on this generation. And there could potentially be long-term adverse outcomes. In 2020, when the lockdowns occurred, they contributed to Wuhan virus-related stress, loneliness, and isolation. Furthermore, many of these adolescents began experiencing "symptoms of depression, anxiety, and then various forms of substance use.

So, cigarette smoking, vaping, alcohol use, and then hard drugs and basically everything we saw that Wuhan virus-related stress, the economic impact on families, the isolation was related to all of that stuff."

Interestingly, the University of Texas Medical Branch researchers in Galveston found that substance use was inversely related. Jeff Temple stated, "The kids who were more likely to stay home and abide by the stay-at-home orders were less likely to use substances. And while that might sound like a positive finding, it isn't because we can't keep kids locked down. So, what that's telling us is that where the kids are getting these substances are hanging out after school or even during school, and so that's something that we need to be mindful of." His conclusions said it "requires us to really listen (and believing them) to our kids and look for changes in them." Other changes would include their choosing to isolate themselves from their peers, wanting to stay at home more, and losing interest in their usual hobbies. His research made them realize that "social interaction is important." He went on to emphasize that parents need to be role models, but it is imperative that their children interact with others, peers, and adults.

There indeed were some advantages that some parents reported. For example, some parents said the restrictions that keep them from going to work, school, the gym, movie theatres, etc., have brought them closer to their loved ones and brought the family members closer together. On the other hand, however, many parents witnessed their children experiencing depressive symptoms and isolation.

The Wuhan virus has given clients more choices on how to receive counseling. No longer is therapy utilized strictly by requiring clients to come to a therapist's office. Now, counseling can also occur through online platforms such as Zoom or FaceTime. In counseling, therapists can teach clients about the benefits of exercise (in any form, including non-strenuous walking), yoga, meditation, and mindfulness to help them through their fears. We still need human interaction and to utilize our support system in addition to how folks initiate counseling and all the recommendations listed above.

When the Wuhan virus first began impacting us, my clients asked how long the virus would last and asked for help with coping skills. Throughout my years as a therapist, I have always used mantras such as "and this too shall pass" and "nothing lasts forever." My clients seemed to focus on everything they couldn't do, while I focused on what we could still do and creatively devised new activities. For example, I am a big music lover, so when I heard that the place where I listened to live music was temporarily closed, the musicians put on a live show and streamed it. We could request songs, and they would play online.

Another example occurred in the Dallas area when the Wuhan virus began impacting its citizens when city officials locked up public tennis courts. This made no sense at all. In playing singles in tennis, if each individual hits tennis balls from the baseline, that is more than exhibiting "social distancing." It didn't take too long for these officials to come to their senses and unlock the chains of these tennis courts. In a further effort to deal with the virus, some folks took the opportunity to learn new skills, such as playing a musical instrument, some joined an online book club, and much more, too numerous to list.

Here are some other remedies for dealing with the impact of the Wuhan virus or any other situation that is creating anxiety: Practice good sleep hygiene and nutrition, stay physically active, utilize one's support system, and not isolate. Listen to soothing music at times for relaxation. In contrast, at other times, find music to dance to that energizes the individual. Other suggestions include remaining emotionally and physically grounded, practicing yoga, deep breathing, relaxation techniques, and mindfulness.

Social Media & Its Impact on Children and Adolescents

Some time ago, there was this observation that an adolescent male and female were sitting at the same table and sitting across from each other. Each was on their respective cell phone, and each was believed to be texting someone else. It turns out they were on a date and texting each other. I am sure this often occurs as adolescent males and females have become so comfortable with texting that face-to-face verbal communication (even when on a date) makes them feel less at ease.

When I used to conduct the presentation "Effective Communication" to federal employees, I emphasized how much more comfortable we have become with non-in-person communication. Instead, we rely on using emails and texting. And with both of these mediums, we are less cautious about what we say or how we say things in our texts or emails. I also gave the following illustration in my presentation. Pretend I am your supervisor, and I am in a hurry to send out an email to all of you. I don't have time to capitalize the first letter for each sentence. Instead, I put the "Caps Lock" on, type my message and send it. Imagine the shock expressed by my audiences when they informed me that my email would imply that I was yelling at them. I replied, so there is such a thing as "email etiquette." And then, I offered this observation: I wanted to know from my audiences who the individual was who came up with the widely held belief that someone who types their email message with the caps locked on is equivalent to yelling at the recipient.

Today, there are so many social media platforms, and the list continues to grow. Here are the most popular sites: Facebook, YouTube, Instagram, Snapchat, Telegram, WhatsApp, WeChat, TikTok, Twitter, Pinterest, and LinkedIn. There are certainly some benefits associated with social networking. All of these sites encourage self-identity, self-expression, community building, and emotional support. Social media has dramatically shifted how we socialize, communicate, and form relationships with each other. But unfortunately, some experts have described social media as being more addictive than cigarettes and alcohol and is now so ingrained in the lives of young people (and maybe adults too).

It is now prudent to discuss how social media has impacted young people's mental health issues. Some of these platforms have young people focusing on their image, which can lead them to have feelings of inadequacy, low self-esteem, and anxiety. Some social media sites allow those who post to have unrealistic expectations and to post their photos. This can quickly make girls and women ashamed of their bodies, so they use filters and edit their pictures to look near-perfect. Spending more than an hour per day on many of these sites can also lead to feelings of loneliness and depression, including difficulty falling and staying asleep. Some cannot establish healthy face-to-face relationships, so they rely on some of these sites to replace what is lacking in their lives.

So, what can a therapist do to help mitigate the adverse effects of social media? The therapist can encourage parents to limit the amount of time a child or adolescent is online, oversee what their child or adolescent is viewing, and initiate a discussion with their offspring if their viewing is distorted or potentially harmful. Suppose the psychotherapist is providing counseling to an underage client. In that case, the therapist can offer some reality testing by encouraging them, giving them opposing information as warranted, and seeking to build their self-esteem. As with the parent, the counselor should encourage the underage client or young adult to reduce time on the internet and these social media sites.

The Effects of Video on Children, Adolescents & Adults

Several researchers have conducted studies to try to understand the effects of video games on the development of children and adolescents. Many types of games are created to achieve different goals – some are entertaining and relaxing. There are other games that are designed to be challenging for learning and brain development.

Today, most games are played online, and many involve multiple players from across the country or around the world, encouraging the child to play with others. This can help children acquire the skills required to work together and solve problems together. In addition, some games function in real-time, and some are fast-paced and require the player to make quick decisions. This helps improve decision-making skills that are valuable in real-life fields, such as sports, where the player needs to make split-second decisions.

By playing video games, kids' hand-eye coordination is essential. Good hand-eye coordination is critical for activities performed on a daily basis. These activities are also required in virtually every sports activity and can even be beneficial in puzzle-solving. When a particular skill is repeated multiple times, the brain develops a structure, and new neural pathways are created, along with transmitters, to optimize its functioning. When intense concentration is applied, the brain is molded to be able to solve problems faster, which can ultimately help them solve issues in real life.

However, not all games are suitable for children, and their effects can be adverse. Kids who spend an excessive amount of time playing video games instead of participating in physical activities can have an adverse impact on the child's health in many ways. For example, a child's cognitive development may be affected if he or she doesn't get out and socialize with peers. In addition, playing video games for long periods of time can lead to obesity and can weaken the muscles and joints. It can also numb hands and fingers due to over-exertion and affect one's eyesight.

The excitement that video games provide is in direct contrast to a typical day in school. As a result, they will prefer video games over anything else, making them inattentive to school work. They may skip homework or decide not to study for tests outside school and choose video games instead of school, which can affect their emotional intelligence.

Many video games contain excessive violence, sexuality, profanity, racism, and many other things that kids cannot perceive correctly. As a result, they may fail to be able to differentiate accurately between the fantasy of the game and may try to emulate the same behavior portrayed in the games. Unfortunately, their brain structure is still developing and may lead to difficulty differentiating right from wrong while they are underage and sometimes not even as adults.

Even though multiplayer games exist, most kids play them alone in their rooms. Unfortunately, this severely limits their real-life interpersonal skills, and they may prefer being alone and interacting through the game. As a result, some kids cannot initiate conversations, and they may feel bored and out of place at social gatherings. And chances are increased that they may be diagnosed with an adjustment disorder, depression, anxiety, and stress. This will undoubtedly impact both their working and personal life.

The violent content and the instant gratification in video games can lead kids to be impatient and aggressive. When things don't go as planned or are restricted by authority figures, they may lash out or start harboring aggressive thoughts that can contribute to troublesome behavior.

So, what are the signs of video game addiction? The first sign of addiction to video games is when the individual becomes defensive and is in denial of the existence of the problem. Next, the child or client may refuse to accept their addiction to video games, even if you provide him with the evidence.

The interest and almost compulsion by the child to continually play video games may lead them to become bored with friends and family. Again, neglecting other activities like studying and connecting with classmates often leads to poor school performance. Some children have difficulty maintaining basic hygiene as well. They may skip baths for days and spend most of their time playing video games.

The child may promise the parent that he will play for a short amount of time, maybe for only 10 minutes or until he finishes a particular level, but he may need more time to be able to follow through and wind up playing for longer hours. All of this can occur without the child even realizing it! The child may exhibit aggressive behavior when he loses the game or fails to complete the level. He may become unreasonably angry and frustrated, unable to understand that it is merely a game.

The parent may end up scolding or prohibiting the child from playing. He will try to find ways to play the game secretly without letting anyone find out. He might start lying or making up excuses to play the game just for a few minutes and continue to push the envelope to pay even longer.

Even when away from the video game, the child will appear distracted and lost in thought, usually thinking about something related to the game or constantly talking about it. Any mention of the gaming addiction may lead the child to become irritated.

There are many pros and cons of video games for children, but parents can put certain limits in place to ensure that their children can enjoy the games without any problems. First, parents should not allow their children to play video games when they are in preschool. Before buying a game, the parent should ensure the game is appropriate for the child by checking the rating, age limit, and content warnings. Next, the parent could try to play the game themself and make themselves a part of their world. By doing so, the child may open up by discussing the various aspects of the game. Next, the parent should instill rules around playing video games and limited playing time. This would include playing games at a friend's place as well.

The parent should keep track of any online interactions their child has with strangers and ensure they do not reveal any personal details to anyone. The parent should keep all the gadgets out of their child's room, especially at night. The parent should make sure the area where the game is played is in public view and can easily spot the screen from afar. The parent is a role model. So, if the parent is also a gamer, the parent needs to enforce the same rules. The parent should only allow their kids to play video games until after they have completed their homework and other tasks. Finally, the parent should ensure the child spends time outdoors and participating in physical activities.

I Wish We Could Return to Simpler Times

This chapter would not be complete without discussing how life has gotten more complicated and stressful for society. Yes, the internet and cell phones, for instance, have given us more immediate access to data and connecting with others. But it has also made us more dependent on these technologies, and the thought of not having access to them even a day might be anxiety-provoking.

I have childhood memories that generations after mine will never be able to experience. For example, I remember summers when my parents informed my siblings and me that they had fed us breakfast and that we should make ourselves scarce until lunch (my parents made the same announcement after lunch). That meant outside activities, throwing a football or a baseball or riding our bikes for hours. I spent a lot of time watching television (after I finished my homework) to shows like Ossie and Harriet, Leave It To Beaver, Father Knows Best, and The Andy Griffith Show. Long before the reputation of Bill Cosby was tarnished or destroyed, as a child, I had purchased all of his comedy albums, and I was a fan of his comedy series, The Cosby Show. What was evident and the common theme in all those shows was how the problems the TV kids were experiencing were resolved at the end of each episode. Values and the concept of right and wrong were on full display in those shows.

Today, we shy away from discussing values, right, and wrong in school and in our society. In school, certain topics are taught that used to be reserved at home (I will let you fill in the blank of what you think parents should teach their children exclusively and not schools). In addition, schools present an alternate view of values that sometimes contrasts with parents. Also, in school, children are exposed to issues such as transgender bathrooms and gender issues. That would include inappropriate books that push a certain agenda to young children and adolescents. The expression "let children be kids" seems to apply here!

To reiterate from Chapter 3, I would welcome a return to a time when subjects like reading, (yes) writing in cursive, arithmetic, and history were taught and emphasized. The teaching of history should not be whitewashed. Even learning historical events that make some feel uncomfortable should also be included. The saying applies: those who do not learn from history are doomed to repeat it. Other subjects should also be taught, such as learning a foreign language, economics, and practical courses like learning to manage one's own finances and the prudent use of credit cards. Unfortunately, common sense has taken a backseat. Today, our educators seem to have an agenda, and their goal appears to take the parents' responsibility in raising their children away from them and instead indoctrinate them to believe that the United States as it was founded was established by white slave owners and the country ought to embrace Communism over Capitalism. My advice to parents would be for them to get involved in how and what their children are taught and to take back their responsibility in raising their offspring. Yes, we, as a society, should indoctrinate our children to teach them right vs. wrong, and it is okay to teach them morals.

One more issue I want to address in this section is the concept that one has to have a college degree to succeed. Many successful individuals have achieved their goals without graduating from college. Furthermore, we, as parents and school counselors, should encourage those who want to pursue a career in which a college degree is unnecessary. Examples include computer technicians, auto mechanics, and other service-related areas.

So, what does all this have to do with counseling? These topics (the Wuhan Virus, social media, video games, and not teaching children values and a sense of right and wrong and not providing clear guard rails) have contributed to our children's and adolescents having to deal with depression, anxiety, low self-esteem, and a lack of self-confidence. It has also made the role of parents in helping their offspring become healthy young adults more challenging. So, it is also evident that our role in providing counseling to children and adolescents and their parents in this current environment has also created additional challenges.

Chapter 6:

The Counseling of Couples and Successful Techniques

When I first began providing counseling to clients, I eventually became confident in working with individuals, but I felt intimidated by marital couples. My fear was that there were two individuals with different opinions, sometimes with different goals, and thus, how was I going to be successful in helping them save their marriage? In addition, at the time, I had not acquired any techniques or exercises in my arsenal to assist them.

6-1

My First Successful Marital Couple

I remember the first couple that put me on the path to gaining confidence in working with marital partners. This couple started the first session by admitting that they had been to several marital therapists in the past, and none had been in the least bit successful with them. They stated that this would probably be the last time they would seek marital counseling, and if I could not help them, they would probably divorce. My first thought was, "No pressure here!" To this day, I am not sure where this approach came from in my head. The following is what I said to them: "I know you have been to several therapists in the past, and I certainly do not want to make the same mistakes that they did. So, if you can, tell me now or if you would like to think about it between now and the next appointment. I would like to know what you can remember about each therapist you saw and what they had to offer. I want to know how they were helpful and if you remember any suggestions they offered. I also want to know how you could not connect with each of them."

During the intake, I not only asked them the usual questions as part of my assessment, but I also asked them how they met, what they remembered about their first date, how they decided to see each other again, how they decided to date each other exclusively, how and why they chose to get married, the attributes they saw in each other then and finally, the strengths of their relationship to balance against their presenting issues. What I learned from their previous counseling was that each therapist had assumed that this couple had acquired skills they didn't actually possess. Hence, the therapists started at a place where this couple could not connect; their techniques went over the couple's heads. So, my hypothesis was to assume that this couple needed the very basics: how to communicate with each other, tell them that conflicts are okay and normal, but it is how to deal with them and not to allow disputes to escalate, techniques such as taking time outs when warranted, etc. So, I addressed each issue and gave them strategies, techniques, and homework assignments to resolve each one. Over time, this couple relayed how the sessions had benefited them. For several years after therapy had ended, the couple kept in touch to inform me that their marriage remained stronger than ever and divorce was never contemplated again.

Over the years, I have found many techniques to strengthen my couples' marriages, such as the homework assignment of getting each partner to make a separate list of past, current, and future activities. Past activities would be those they used to enjoy together, but they stopped the activity for some reason, but now, they might consider bringing the activity back into their marriage. Present activities would be those noted that they would like to continue together and are satisfying to them. Future activities are ones that they have never done together, but they believe they would be enjoyable. They could be activities from "A Bucket List" (activities that a marital partner hopes the couple might do at least once during their marriage). My personal example from my own bucket list is my hope that my wife could attend the 4 Grand Slams in tennis: the US Open, Wimbledon, the French Open, and the Australian Open.

I encourage all couples to have date nights at least once a week. While on the date night, the couple cannot talk about their work, their children's schedule, household responsibilities, bills, etc. So, what is permissible? They can talk about how they met; their first impressions of each other on their first date, reasons why they decided to see each other again after that first date, why they chose not to date anyone else and to see each other exclusively, why they decided to marry their significant other, memorable dates, vacations, holidays, attributes they found and continue to find endearing. Another suggestion would be for the couple to consider reliving their first date, a memorable anniversary, when and where they became engaged, etc.

I also believe it is helpful for each partner to divide their lives into equal parts, not including work. One part is their marriage; as stated before, every couple should have that date night every week to continue bonding. Another part of the equation is time spent with their children, their spouse, or each partner having individual quality time with their child or children. The last part of the equation is their personal interests, needs, and pursuits. For example, I enjoy hitting tennis balls with a friend for at least 2 hours. Although this was how my wife and I met, she is no longer interested in playing tennis; she gives her blessings to me, knowing this provides pleasure to me. She has her own interests, from bicycling to knitting, and I encourage her to pursue those interests and hobbies. What I am trying to say is that it is okay to have different interests, even healthy (of course, so long as their interests and pursuits are not contrary to the monogamy of their marriage). When a couple gets married, each partner does not have to give up what they enjoy, and each partner does not have to conform to their partner's interests if they choose not to.

Many couples express the amount of "work" required to keep their marriage/relationship satisfying. So, I would ask them how much effort or "work" was needed when they first met and began dating. They would reply there wasn't much effort required at all. They would explain that it was fun sharing common interests with someone they were attracted to and getting to know each other by asking a lot of questions. I would then suggest that no matter how long they have been together, they should continue asking questions and continue learning about their partner. It is a myth to believe that we know everything about our partner as time passes. It is true that over the years, each of us changes (our priorities, perhaps our goals, while the core within us remains constant). If this is true for ourselves, then it is true for our significant other.

For that reason, I suggest to my counseling couples that they could play a game from the 1970s called the "Newlywed Game," where they try to guess how their significant other would answer questions posed by their partner. They could play this game while taking walks together, over dinner, or just spending a quiet night at home. Then they could act on the answers provided by their partner. For example, let's say one spouse asks the other who their favorite musical artist is. Then that spouse learns their partner's favorite performer is coming to town and surprising their significant other by purchasing tickets to their concert. Again, the purpose of this exercise is to prove that no matter how much a partner believes they know about their significant other, they will be surprised when they discover facts they never knew and have fun in the process. As a result of this exercise and others, the opportunities to continue to bond with each other are boundless.

I have a similar experience to relay. When my wife-to-be and I were dating and getting to know each other, she revealed that her favorite event was watching ice skating during the Winter Olympics. A few months later, I discovered the Ice Capades were coming to town. I took the initiative by purchasing tickets and asked her to share some of her favorite restaurants with me. I surprised her by taking her to one of her favorite restaurants and to the Ice Capades performance. She said at the time that she had no idea what I had planned for the evening. Hint: Both men and women love surprises! When surprises are acted upon, that partner is making a massive deposit in their loved one's "Love Bank!"

The whole emphasis is to keep the relationship exciting, even in the smallest ways, to continue to make each other feel important and special. There doesn't have to be any cost involved at all. For example, they could write each other love notes and put them on the front seat of their car or their significant other's lunch that they may take to work, or leave "I love you," "I miss you," and "I can't wait to see you soon." text messages to each other during the workday. The purpose is to not take each other for granted and continue to find ways to show them that you care and love them. These suggestions can be offered to your eventual marital couple clients.

Often, I have recommended to couples that for intimacy to occur in the bedroom, it first needs to happen outside the bedroom. Sometimes, men will reply, "Great, that means we can have sex throughout the house!" To these men, I will then need to define intimacy as not just about sex. Intimacy, in addition to sex, is also about displays of affection, holding hands, putting your arms around each other, a peck on the cheek or a kiss on the lips, and, again, telling each other how much you love them.

Now, I want to address an exercise for individuals who are not married and wonder if the significant other they are considering marrying and/or being in a long-term relationship meets their long-term needs. I will ask the individual to list major headings and separate sheets of paper. They would include physical attributes, personality, intelligence, temperament, shared interests, common values, etc. I will ask the individual to make the list as comprehensive as possible. They can add to the list as they consider more items. Then, the individual can review the list and prioritize the entries. They can note that some of the items or attributes are non-negotiable, meaning that their significant other must possess that particular attribute, such as being of the same religion or culture. Part of the assignment's purpose is for individuals not to settle for someone who doesn't meet their needs. Sometimes, individuals hurry into a relationship for fear that another one may not come their way if they pass on this relationship. Or an individual may enter into a relationship out of loneliness.

Many believe that when one falls in love with someone, the feeling of love comes exclusively from the heart. I contend that it is actually the head telling the heart to "fall in love," It is the head informing the heart that there is a match between the attributes we seek and traits that the person we seek possesses.

6-2 Example of A Male Client Repeatedly Settling

Many years ago, I was counseling a male who was in his early 60s. His presenting issue was fear of growing old and being alone. He explained he had been married and divorced multiple times. Other times, he had been in other relationships that resulted in moving in and out of each other's residences. Finally, there were occasions when he and another were dating exclusively for a while before breaking up for one reason or another. But none of his marriages or relationships ever lasted beyond ten years. As we discussed his history, I discovered that he had never "played the field" (in his case, dating any women without intending to have sex with any of them). Instead, he had pursued one woman at a time based on their physical attractiveness to him. Then, he would take the relationship as far as it would go. Since each relationship was based on physical beauty, it often led to physical intimacy before the other attributes were explored: common interests, values, intelligence, etc.

So, I began counseling him by using a particular discussion. It worked so well that I started using it with other clients. The discussion was about how healthy relationships form. I emphasized that the factors involved are no different at the beginning from how healthy friendships occur. Below is the illustration I shared with this client.

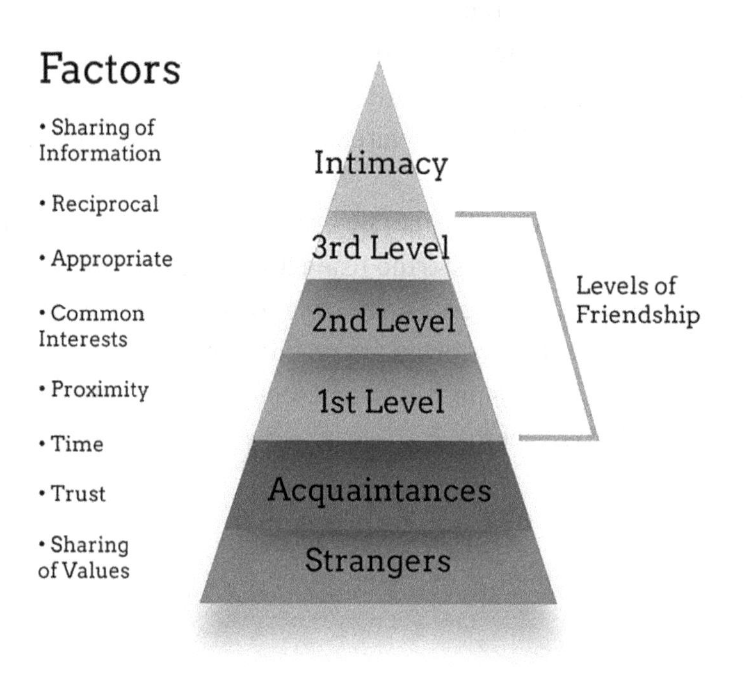

As you can see, at the bottom of the triangle is the word "strangers," which denotes that most of the individuals we encounter are strangers. An example would be two individuals who have been called for jury duty and end up sitting next to each other. If they begin a conversation, the topics would be chitchat and often around the only activity they share in common, which is being called for jury duty. For example, one person may mention that they have never been called for jury duty, while the other informs the first that they have been called and have served on a jury many times. In every context, appropriate boundaries are essential. Usually, one does not reveal too much about themselves, as the thought is, "I will probably never see this person again.

So, in this phase, two individuals may share information, and hopefully, sharing information is appropriate. Maybe the other person will reciprocate, and what they share again is appropriate. However, if what they share is not suitable to the situation, there is usually a voice inside each of us that says, "Run like hell; this person has no boundaries." An example from the scenario mentioned above is where one individual is not adhering to healthy boundaries and says, "Gee, I hope it won't be discovered that there is a warrant out for my arrest for all those unpaid speeding tickets during this jury duty."

If two individuals progress to the next healthy friendship/relationship level, they enter into the "acquaintance" phase. An example would be two people working for the same company. The only commonality they share is their work. Perhaps scant personal information about each other is shared, such as marital status, whether they have children, maybe what part of town they reside in, and perhaps their hobbies when they aren't working. This exchange of information still keeps them in the acquaintance phase. They are still acquaintances even if they discover they share a hobby and pursue it together. Before individuals move from one level to the next, the factor of "time" needs to occur if "trust" is to be established. It would be silly if one were to say to another, "Yesterday I didn't trust you, but today I do."

The first time an individual shares something revealing about themselves, there is hope that the other person will accept the information without judgment. It also takes time for each individual to know that trust has been established. Trust occurs over time when each person reveals a little piece of information about themselves and the other party without judgment or criticism and maintains the secrets that have been shared.

The next phase is the 1st Level of Friendship. In this phase, two people must have shared reciprocal information about themselves, and at this level, they discover that they share common interests. They want to engage in that activity together, and time has allowed some level of trust to occur. Let's go back to the example of two people working together. Let's say they discover that they share a common interest aside from their work, such as playing tennis or the same kind of music. What is also important at this level is their proximity to each other. Of course, they could decide to do something together after work, so proximity is not as important. But if they choose to partake in their shared interest on the weekend, for instance, where each resides could make a difference, assuming they live 30 miles or greater from each other.

The following two levels are the 2nd and 3rd levels of friendship. All the previous factors exemplify this: sharing of information, reciprocal, appropriate at each level, sharing common interests, including time and trust. If an individual reveals something and it is met with judgment, then the friendship will either be frozen at that level or revert to a lower one. Another factor occurs at the upper levels of friendship—the agreement of shared values. It could be religious beliefs political beliefs or morals, etc.

The last level of achieving a healthy friendship/relationship is intimacy, and in this context, I am not talking about physical intimacy. If two people were to reveal the most intimate information about themselves, who would they feel the most comfortable doing so? It could be their marital partner, a friend of 10 years or more, or perhaps a sibling. Two people who achieved this level did so by accomplishing all other previous factors: sharing appropriate information, reciprocation, having common interests, proximity, time, trust, and shared values.

If we were to discuss the attributes of a healthy relationship headed toward marriage or had achieved that, we would see that the healthiest ones had accomplished a healthy friendship first. And this resembles the triangle that was illustrated above, where if physical intimacy does occur, it might be wise to wait until they have achieved the upper part of the triangle. This would likely not happen until at least the 3rd level of friendship or intimacy phase of the friendship. Before physical intimacy occurs, one or both individuals might ask, "Do we want to take our friendship/relationship to the next level and become sexually intimate?'

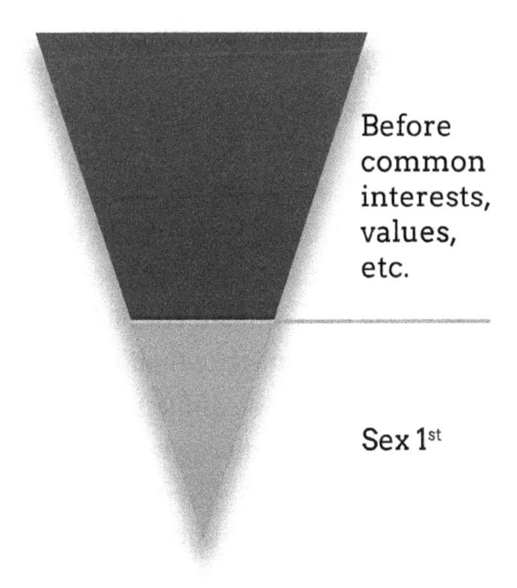

The illustration above resembles an upside-down triangle where sex is introduced early on before all the traits of a healthy friendship are established first. In this context, one individual might say to the other, "We are good in bed together; what else do we have in common?" This doesn't mean that successful relationships and/or marriages can't survive from this example, but let's go back to the 60-year-old client I discussed earlier. If he had taken the time to establish a healthy friendship first, perhaps his outcome would have yielded what he was searching for: a marriage that would last and where he and his partner shared common interests, values, goals, etc. As a result, they could grow old together and achieve a happy, satisfying marriage.

I want to share another couple's story with you, where sometimes you, as a therapist, must postpone marital counseling to deal with a spouse's issues.

6-3 Another Marital Couple Example

A couple presented themselves for marital counseling. As always, I began by asking them how I could be of assistance. Each looked at the other to see who would speak first. Finally, the husband said, "We experienced conflicts before we married, and I thought those conflicts would disappear once we married." I explored what those conflicts were and how they attempted to resolve them. I discovered that the husband would avoid discussing disputes when a conflict occurred. I further asked about the husband's upbringing and how his parents dealt with disputes. He admitted that his parents never resolved their disagreements and avoided them. I shared with them that conflicts in marriage and life are unavoidable. In an attempt to add humor, I said, "Confucius says those who sweep issues under the carpet wind up with lumpy carpet." After a few sessions of attempting to help them with their marital issues, it became apparent that the husband needed individual therapy to recognize and accept that when his parents avoided disputes, they were never or rarely resolved. I met with the husband for a few personal appointments and succeeded in assisting him to accept that conflicts are normal. Then we resumed marital therapy and succeeded in helping the couple enhance their ability to communicate their feelings and discuss and resolve their disputes.

So, what are some of the secrets of a successful marriage? First, spouses in these marriages do not consider or talk about divorce, even when angry. They are committed to their marriage, and divorce is not an option. Partners in successful marriages like and respect each other before and after marriage. They have friends within the union, and each has nonsexual friends who can satisfy their interests/hobbies. Suppose an individual does not have parents who were role models for a happy marriage. In that case, they seek out those who have an exemplary marriage and ask them many questions about what has made their marriage successful.

Spouses are not going to be in love with each other all the time. Throughout their marriage, they may want and need to recapture the magic, the mystique. In that case, they need to be loving toward each other. They will need to repeat behaviors and verbalizations that led them to fall in love, such as initiating holding hands, giving each other hello and goodbye kisses and kisses for no reason at all, and telling each other often, "I love you." The expression seems appropriate here, "Fake it till you make it." By continuing to repeat positive behaviors and verbalizations, it is possible that love can be re-established again as it once was at the beginning of their relationship. There are books that have been written to help partners bond, such as "1001 Ways To Be Romantic" by Gregory J. P. Godek. I not only have this book on my shelf in my private practice office, but I also have a copy at home. For the couples I see, I often show them the book and suggest they implement the author's suggestions frequently. I also encourage couples to come up with their romantic ideas befitting their own relationship.

Over the years, I have read many self-help books from colleagues and attended many seminars on helping couples succeed in their relationships. Often, they say or write that they will "teach couples how to fight fair." Suppose we were to poll the general population; who would define "fight" or "fighting" therapeutically? So, it would require those authors and those conducting these seminars to redefine "fighting" in different ways and what constitutes "fair fighting." If I were to follow their recommendations, I would thus imagine myself as a referee in a boxing ring with a couple I am counseling. I would have a penalty flag and a whistle and use them for "illegal fighting." This is not where I want to be. I do not want to be the arbiter of "legal versus Illegal fighting."

So, I encourage couples to avoid using the word "fighting" in their relationship. If their mate has said something hurtful, I encourage them to discuss the feeling without acting out their anger and retaliating verbally or behaviorally. Instead, they can tell their partner that what was said or done was hurtful. Finally, when talking about and looking to resolve a conflict, each partner has an opinion that is neither right nor wrong. It is just an opinion. If each is trying to prove who is right and wrong, that is a losing proposition to the relationship. For no one wants to hear they were wrong. The goal of resolving a conflict is to understand the issues, understand the other's viewpoint(s), and agree on which option(s) will be the best to implement, sometimes by one yielding to their mate's viewpoint or seeking a compromise. To succeed in a healthy relationship, they must relinquish their ego and pride. They seek what is in their union's best interest; thus, they could yield to their partner's opinion if theirs is more favorable to their goals.

I believe it is essential to establish ground rules for couples to follow in and out of session. Again, the therapist must ensure that neither partner feels "picked on" during each session, and at the end of each session, I want them to confirm this. Also, at the end of each session, I will ask the couple if this is a good place to stop. I may ask each by name to confirm. They cannot say that this was a good place to end and then admonish each other outside the session for what each of them said during the appointment. I would obtain their agreement during their initial session.

Another ground rule to ensure couples adhere to is what they can and cannot discuss between sessions. In a positive way, they can acknowledge how well the appointment went and praise each other for all wanted behavior between sessions. I want my couples to enjoy their quality time together through "dates" and during mealtimes. They would at least give each other a goodnight kiss; they could cuddle and spend quality time talking when they get into bed together and drifting off to sleep. Certainly, physical intimacy is not discouraged. If a topic cannot be resolved between sessions, they should agree to bring the issue to counseling before it escalates into an argument. At each appointment, the couple will practice communication skills in the session, which will help them resolve each issue. As the couple progresses, I offer a lot of praise to the couple, utilizing the tools and skills they have learned. My goal with every couple and client is to work myself out of a job with each of them.

The last issue I want to bring up for discussion is about expectations and "shoulds." Every partner needs to praise each other for all desired behaviors, even if that endeavor has been praised 1000 times before; it never hurts to complement each other again and again. Honoring each other for behaviors they want to continue ensures that each partner does not take the other for granted. Except for agreements that neither will be unfaithful to the other or spend the relationship into the poor house, the partners ought to consider letting go of expectations.

Along with letting go of expectations, we might consider eliminating "shoulds" from our vocabulary. I don't know how new it is, but there is an expression, "Don't should on yourself or your significant other!" "Shoulds" make it appear like there are high bars for our partner or us that we ought to live up to, and if the bar is not met, we are greatly disappointed in ourselves or others.

Over the years, I have collected and posted sayings on bulletin boards in my private practice office for couples to view. Here is one: "Touch each other (holding hands, putting your arms around each other, etc.). Show affection, make friends with other couples, praise each other, be thankful, enjoy time away from each other with your interests and hobbies, which makes the heart grow fonder, and don't try to keep up with the Jones-enjoy what you have. Enjoy the simple pleasures together, such as cooking, having a picnic, and lying in a hammock together. Saving money toward long-term mutual goals. Think positive, be positive."

Here are other suggestions for couples: be committed to each other, focus on their chemistry and compatibility, seek to improve their communication, be caring and affectionate toward each other, give attention to each other, and accept each other without trying to change them. After all, this is what led them to fall in love with one another in the first place.

I am a fan of the TV series "Blue Bloods," and when the characters, "Jamie" and "Eddie," were announcing their engagement to the other Reagan family members, they shared their vows. "I will always have your back. If you fall behind, I will wait up. I will earn your respect and pay you with respect every day we have. I will be your scout and night watchman, your calvary, your medic, your chaplain in our army of two. No retreat, no surrender. You can count on me." When appropriate, I have encouraged couples to develop their vows and commitments to each other.

This chapter would not be complete without discussing the clinician's role in encouraging marital couples to stay together and adhere to their marital vows, especially if they have children. Of course, a counselor can point out that it is not as critical if the union has produced no children and decides to end their relationship. There are occasions when divorce is warranted, such as domestic abuse.

If a couple is declaring irreconcilable differences, then I believe it is important to explain to the couple that if there is a child or children from their union, in most cases, they do better in school and life if the couple is able to resolve their marital issues. Counseling can be the vehicle that can assist the couple in achieving a happy and satisfying marriage and overcoming those stated differences. Therefore, I will emphasize just how crucial it is that they put all their efforts and allow a therapist to assist them in accomplishing their marital goals, not only for their marriage's sake, but also for their children's sake.

I found the following statistics from a website called "Fix Family Courts," and the article is entitled "Fatherless Single Mother Home Statistics." When appropriate, I share these statistics with parents. "Kids From Single-Parent Homes are 5 times more likely to attempt to take their own life, 6 times more likely to be in poverty, 9 times more likely to drop out of high school, 10 times more likely to abuse alcohol and/or drugs, 20 times more likely to go to prison and 32 times more likely to run away from home."

I began this chapter by admitting that marital counseling was an area where I was not confident at the beginning of my career. However, I have found success in working with couples using some of the techniques presented in this chapter. As I became more confident and competent, I actually enjoy providing counseling to couples. I have found that in working with couples, as with any population, the goal is to find fun techniques that clients enjoy completing and, at the same time, yield favorable results. I encourage fellow clinicians to try some or all of these techniques presented or feel free to find ones that fit with your counseling style.

CHAPTER 7:

Finding Success in Working With Affective Disorders, Substance Abuse & Schizophrenics

AGAIN, I WAS fortunate enough to work at the Wichita Falls Mental Health Mental Retardation Center, where I began my career. I was trained to complete comprehensive intake assessments for the first two years. The Center also had a psychiatrist on staff and was in our building. This psychiatrist and I had established an excellent working relationship. Sometimes, he would even allow me to sit in on his assessments when I had referred a patient to him. Then, after completing his evaluation and the patient had left, I would ask why he chose one medication over another and ask other medication-related questions. Over time, I became very confident in assessing depression, bipolar, and anxiety and learning about the various medications to treat these disorders.

Depression

Whenever I have assessed an individual throughout my career, I have always tried to determine if the individual met the criteria for situational depression vs. depression due to a chemical imbalance. If the client were experiencing symptoms directly due to a specific situation, I would suggest that counseling be initiated first and postpone a referral to a psychiatrist to consider an antidepressant. It is not because I am not in favor of antidepressants but because my role as a therapist is to teach clients healthy coping skills. I have often told clients that antidepressants cannot teach them anything about coping skills. If I am successful and the client's depressive symptoms improve, the goal was accomplished without using an antidepressant. Sometimes, though, counseling alone may not be successful in alleviating the symptoms, and the client's depression does not improve. Below is an actual scenario that occurred while employed at the Wichita Falls MHMR Center, where I had to refer a depressed client to a psychiatrist for an antidepressant.

7-1 Depression Case Example

During the intake with a female client, she expressed moderate symptoms of depression that included difficulty motivating herself, a loss of interest in usual hobbies, a decrease in her ability to concentrate, and a reduction in her productivity at work. There were no suicidal ideations; this was the first time the client experienced depressive symptoms. The client revealed that the symptoms began shortly after her fiancé broke off the engagement with her. So, it was evident that her depression was situational. The client and I agreed that we would try counseling for four sessions. Then, if the symptoms did not improve, we would consider a referral to a psychiatrist for a possible antidepressant. With each session, I used all kinds of strategies, metaphors, and analogies; all my attempts and methods went over her head each time. After the 4th session, it was agreed to refer her to a psychiatrist, and an antidepressant was prescribed while I continued to provide therapy. It took a few weeks for the antidepressant to begin improving her symptoms. Then, she suddenly could comprehend what I was trying to convey in one session. It was almost like she was saying, "Oh, that is what you have been trying to say to me. Now I get it." Counseling continued along with the antidepressant long enough to alleviate the symptoms, and I continued to teach her those healthy coping skills. So, a successful therapist must be flexible and adaptable and continuously assess what changes need to occur to achieve the client's goals. In this case, I suggested we consider bringing in a psychiatrist to assist us, and the client accepted that recommendation.

There are many forms of depression and bipolar, and it would be helpful to share them for discussion. Let's start with depression. There is Major Depression, either Single Episode or Recurrent. There are, of course, criteria that need to be met with these diagnoses, which would include five or more symptoms, such as a depressed mood that is evident nearly every day, markedly diminished interest or pleasure in a client's usual activities, either a significant weight gain or weight loss in a month, either insomnia or hypersomnia nearly every day, either psychomotor agitation or retardation almost every day, fatigue or a loss of energy nearly every day, feelings of worthlessness and/or excessive guilt, diminished ability to concentrate, think or make decisions almost every day, recurrent thoughts of death and/or suicidal ideations with or without a specific plan.

Another depressive disorder to cover is called Dysthymic Disorder, which is indicative of a depressed mood for most of the day, if not every day, for at least two years. Dysthymia is a milder yet more chronic form of Major Depression. In addition to a depressed mood, the individual must have two or more symptoms present: poor appetite or overeating, insomnia or hypersomnia, low energy or fatigue, low self-esteem, poor concentration and/or making decisions, and feelings of hopelessness. The symptoms are not as severe to diagnose Major Depression, either Single Episode or Recurrent.

Now, let's turn our attention to clients who meet the criteria to be diagnosed with a Bipolar Disorder. The symptoms of a manic episode are a distinct period of abnormally or elevated, expansive, or irritable mood lasting at least one week. Other symptoms would include (three or more) inflated self-esteem or grandiosity, decreased need for sleep (feeling rested after only 3 hours of sleep or ability to stay awake for a day or days at a time), more talkative than usual, or a pressure to keep talking, flight of ideas (the client is bouncing from one thought to another and listeners are not able to find a connection from one idea to another) and client admitting to racing thoughts. The client is easily distracted, has an abundance of goals they have set, but has difficulty accomplishing any of them because they jump from one activity to another. The client may have an excessive involvement in pleasurable activities that have a high potential for painful consequences, such as extreme buying sprees, foolish business ventures, investments, or traffic tickets for reckless driving or speeding tickets.

For all diagnoses of Major Depression, Dysthymia, and Bipolar most mental health experts believe they are a result of chemical imbalances in the brain. However, this area still needs further research on how these chemical imbalances affect these disorders. In addition, many mental health professionals believe that the diagnoses of Adjustment Disorder with Anxiety, Adjustment Disorder with Depressed Mood, and Adjustment Disorder with Mixed Depressive Mood and Anxiety are not indicative of a chemical imbalance but are examples of situations or circumstances that lead toward these distinctions.

Let's continue to discuss the use of antidepressants. We have already discussed that there are clients whose depression is not situational. They have had bouts of depression throughout their life without a situation. Also, there is a history of other family members diagnosed with depression. This is an example of why a thorough assessment is vital. Therefore, a clinician needs to inform these individuals that they may have a chemical imbalance and may need to be on an antidepressant for the rest of their life.

Did you know that there is a phenomenon known as "Antidepressant Poopout?" The medical term is called tachyphylaxis. Let's say a client has been on antidepressant medication like Prozac for some years, and it has been very effective in controlling the symptoms. But over time, the drug becomes less effective. That is called the Poopout effect. So, a psychiatrist has other antidepressants to choose from when one medication "poopouts." Here is an interesting tidbit: Just because an antidepressant pooped out in the past, it could still be used sometime in the future and can be just as effective as it once was.

There is something else I want to bring up as part of the discussion about antidepressants. There has been a lot of debate about whether taking an antidepressant contributes to or causes one to begin having suicidal ideations. This seems to defy logic. How can a medication that is supposed to reduce or alleviate symptoms of depression cause or contribute to suicidal ideations? Let me offer two possible explanations. First, another sign is low energy when an individual is severely depressed with suicidal ideations. They are so depressed that they might attempt suicide, but they don't have the energy to follow through. So, the patient is assessed and put on an antidepressant. One of the first symptoms that may improve when starting the medication is that the drug may give the client more energy. So, you now have a patient who is still severely depressed and still has suicidal ideations but now has the energy to attempt or succeed in taking their life.

The following is the other possible explanation for why an individual may attempt or take their life while on an antidepressant, and the act is blamed on the medication. Say an individual started on an antidepressant and then finds out it wasn't effective or it wasn't working fast enough. So, in both examples, it was the medications that were blamed. But the question to ask is whether the antidepressants led patients to attempt or follow through on taking their life. In both instances, individuals who are severely depressed with suicidal ideations should be admitted into a psychiatric facility and put on suicidal watch when the antidepressant medication is introduced. Then, keep the patient on alert until the ideations pass.

If you were to look up all the warnings about antidepressant medications, you would find what is referred to as "black box warnings," indicating that they were associated with an increased risk of suicidal thinking, feeling, and behavior in patients in which these medications were prescribed. It seems plausible that these warnings protect the drug manufacturers from potential lawsuits and that the public and prescribers were warned about the potential risks. So, again, it seems prudent to refer all clients with major depression with suicidal ideations to a psychiatric hospital before an antidepressant medication is prescribed. Then, the patient will remain in the hospital until the suicidal ideations no longer persist.

It is vital to continue to mention that the process is the same with every client or couple. The mental picture I have with each is imagining the issues they bring to counseling is like jigsaw puzzle pieces. Then, collaboratively, we put the pieces together by asking the questions, like the TV character Columbo. Again, I always ask every client/couple what goals they want to accomplish, which becomes our road map. So, of course, that is my agenda when meeting with someone with depressive symptoms or any other presenting issue.

As a cognitive-behavioral therapist, I use visualizations, metaphors, analogies, and logical, common-sensical ways to communicate my points. Below is an illustration I use with clients to show how our "self-talk is responsible for the resulting emotions we experience:

Events/People
Self-Talk Mind
Resulting Mood(s)/Emotions

I define "Events" and "People" to my clients. "If I ask you to tell me about an Event, I only want you to tell me about (the Event) what has occurred without telling me how you felt about the Event. I only want you to give me the facts about the Event and nothing more." The same can be said about "People"- "I only want you to tell me what someone said and did and nothing more." One thing that makes us human is that we all talk to ourselves (and it is okay to admit that we all speak to ourselves) so that when an event has occurred or someone has said or done something, it triggers in our mind to have Self Talk. Our self-talk can either be positive or negative. And our self-talk guides us to an emotion or a mood like a rudder steers a boat. Here is an example: most people would consider being laid off from one's job as a negative event. If they saw it as a negative event, so would their self-talk (negative), and to be consistent, so would their resulting moods and emotions (negative). However, one does not have to see the Event as being negative. For example, an individual could see the Event (being laid off) as a blessing in disguise, and their resulting self-talk could be, "Good interviewing skills got me this job, so the next job I accept, I will make sure it is less stressful."

Clinicians can also use this illustration of negative and positive self-talk to help clients understand the connection between their self-talk and their self-esteem. Positive self-talk can also be used to bolster one's self-esteem, while negative self-talk chips away at their self-esteem and self-confidence. For example, I saw this quote from Toby Mac, a musician who focuses on Christian hip-hop and rock, "Sometimes you have to tell the negative committee that meets inside your head to just sit down and shut up."

Some additional suggestions that can help alleviate depression symptoms. One recommendation is to encourage our clients to exercise and define what exercise is and how encompassing it is. Any movement is exercise, from walking, running, taking the stairs, dancing, etc. Just 30 minutes of exercise a day! In addition, exercise can also increase one's metabolism and aid in weight loss, blood circulation, digestion, and self-image. Finally, it can help relieve stress, allow clients to fall and stay asleep, help improve the client's thinking skills (including concentration, problem-solving, and decision-making skills), reduce headaches and chronic pain, and reduce Alzheimer's.

I have clients imagine that there is a gnome sitting on each shoulder. One gnome is encouraging the client to cease doing anything and everything to benefit them. For example, if you don't want to get out of bed, don't; if they choose not to shower or take care of their hygiene, don't; if they decide not to exercise, don't, etc. The other gnome is sitting on the other shoulder and is suggesting to the client that if they follow the recommendations from the other gnome, they will not feel better. For instance, the only way we obtain a second wind (an increase in energy) is to expend energy. Therefore, clients must force themselves to accomplish what the depression is encouraging them to do and to wallow in their symptoms. So, if I can get a client to push themselves to get out of bed, shower, take a 30-minute walk, etc., they will admit they feel better at the end of the day. Each successful day strings together, reducing their depressive symptoms and improving their self-esteem, even without the need for an antidepressant.

It is important to note that there are at least a couple of ways for clients to improve their self-esteem. One way is to change their self-talk from negative to positive. Another way is through a sense of accomplishment. The more goals (short and long term) they achieve (sometimes forcing themselves), their self-esteem, self-image, and confidence will improve.

Speaking of self-esteem and depression, I once read an article from Reader's Digest that came from author and psychiatrist David Burns in his book, "Feeling Good: The New Mood Therapy." If your best friend knocked on your door and informed you that they had lost their job, their marriage was in trouble, and they needed a place to stay, you would offer them your home. You would help to bolster their self-esteem and self-confidence. You would help to correct their negative self-talk because, after all, this individual is your best friend. So, Burns went on to say, why do we not always treat ourselves as our own best friend? Because, after all, we have to live with ourselves. That would mean correcting our negative self-talk to bolster our self-esteem and counter depressive symptoms.

Bipolar

The following case stands out while working at the MHMR Center in Wichita Falls.

7-2 Bipolar Case Example

I was conducting an assessment with a woman who admitted to symptoms of depression and had no problems, wanting a referral to our staff psychiatrist for an antidepressant prescription. However, as I conducted a comprehensive evaluation, the client made me suspect that she might be manic-depressive. Rather than revealing to her my suspected diagnosis of bipolar or manic depression, I decided to ask her about the symptoms of mania. And yes, for every sign of depression, she also had experienced, at times, symptoms of mania. Her manic symptoms included a decreased need for sleep and feeling super creative. Her ability to concentrate and focus improved (even though she was easily distracted and had difficulty maintaining her focus). She had the belief that she could accomplish many tasks, including an increase in her ability to set and achieve goals, as well as having an inflated self-esteem, being more sociable with others, and having more energy, all during these periods of mania. When the client admitted to these symptoms of mania, she emphatically said she did not want any medication to stop her highs, only the lows. As I pressed her, she also disclosed that she often could not harness her concentration and was easily distracted. She was able to start projects, but before she completed one, she would initiate another and rarely completed any. She also had flights of ideas where others were having problems following her train of thought. And finally, she admitted to buying sprees, making foolish business decisions, and even reckless driving.

I had to inform her that treating her bipolar symptoms was not like going through a buffet line where she could pick and choose which traits she wanted to acquire. They were all part of the package. Finally, I convinced her to see our psychiatrist (with me accompanying her) and allowed him to fully assess her for both depression and mania. At the end of the evaluation, we persuaded her that she possessed bipolar symptoms and that the appropriate medication was prescribed. In addition to a bipolar med being prescribed, I continued to provide counseling to her to teach relevant coping skills and encourage her to continue taking her medication as prescribed for the rest of her life.

There are times when a female might temporarily exhibit bipolar symptoms. For example, increased estrogen levels during menstruation, pregnancy, and menopause can trigger manic symptoms. It is also possible that once these hormones are stabilized, for instance, after the birth of an infant, the symptoms can be abated. In addition, stressful life events, such as the death of a loved one, divorce, or job loss, can trigger bipolar symptoms. A psychiatrist could put an individual on medication for a short time and then slowly wean the person off to ensure the symptoms don't return. However, in most individuals, once the diagnosis of bipolar has occurred, and it is not situational, and medication is warranted, that client/patient will more than likely need to remain on a bipolar med for the rest of their life.

The difficulty of working with manic-depressive or bipolar clients is getting them to remain on their medication. Either they don't like how the drug makes them feel, or they miss the highs they experience when they are in a manic phase. Therefore, it is helpful to have the client list on paper the manic symptoms they were experiencing before the medication was prescribed and how the drug has now stabilized them and led them to balance the two extremes. Then, as clients consider ceasing the med, I would encourage them to look at the list as to why the med was needed in the first place.

Since we are discussing medication and the bipolar client, if the physician believes the individual cycles between depression and mania, an antidepressant should not be prescribed alone, as it can trigger a manic episode. The physician would prescribe both an antidepressant and either a mood stabilizer or an antipsychotic to control both the depression and the manic symptoms. Once the individual is stabilized on the correct medication, then psychotherapy (CBT or family-focused therapy) will be more effective. Along with medication and psychotherapy, as with all clients, encourage them to exercise (which can improve their depression), do yoga, meditate, and follow a healthy diet.

One more issue that needs to be addressed regarding the bipolar patient is their tendency to use or abuse either alcohol or substances as a way of self-medicating. Until recently, psychiatrists would not prescribe medication to bipolar patients until they ceased self-medicating. However, now psychiatrists see the efficacy of treating both concurrently.

Anxiety

As a cognitive-behavioral therapist, I apply strategies and techniques that are the most logical and common-sensical. And I am also very consistent. So, I often use the concept of positive and negative "Self-talk" to explain why we experience positive and negative emotions. I use the following visualization as well. Imagine, if you will, that we are sponges when it comes to absorbing emotions or energy, whether they are positive or negative. Absorbing positive emotions (love, happiness, contentment, self-confidence, etc.) and positive energy are okay. However, absorbing negative emotions (depression, anxiety, guilt, jealousy, etc.) or energy is not okay. So, as an individual/ client recognizes a negative emotion is headed their way and could be absorbed like a sponge, they could imagine a shield on their arm, deflecting the negative emotion away from them. Like a laser beam, they would decide upon a "plan of action" to resolve the source of their negative emotion.

Another way to illustrate how our negative self-talk leads to anxiety is to visualize a "V." Below is that illustration:

How Self-Talk Impacts Anxiety

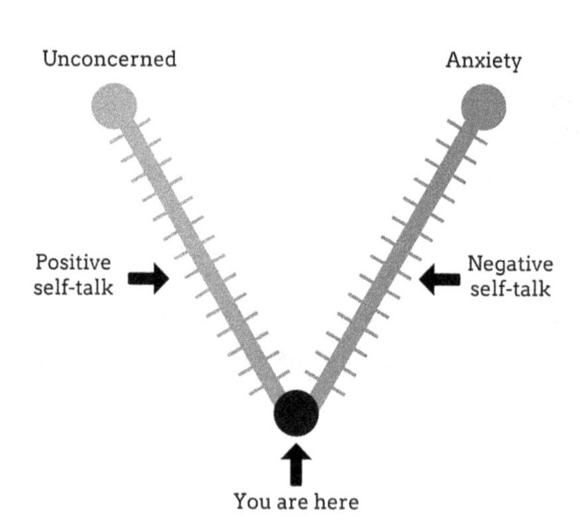

As you can see from the illustration above, the notches on each side of the "V" indicate our self-talk. On the right side of the "V" reveals negative self-talk. At any point in time, an individual can observe that if they do not change their self-talk at the top of the "V," it will lead to anxiety. Therefore, the individual can reverse course, return to "Here

You Are," and take the left path. Down this path is where the individual ensures their self-talk is positive. And at the end of this path, at the top of the "V," are emotions such as "Unconcerned" or "Unworried." Again, we choose whether our self-talk will be positive or negative.

Often, individuals will engage in negative "what-ifs," which also contributes to anxiety. Here is an example of what-ifs from a client who came in for assistance.

7-3 A Client's Use What Ifs

I had already seen this client for anxiety, and she proceeded to share the following scenario. Her brother-in-law had a set of medical symptoms. These symptoms indicated that the diagnosis could be either a medical condition that could be easily treated with medication or a diagnosis with a very bleak prognosis. The client said she was sure the diagnosis would eventually be confirmed as the worst one. When asked how she knew that, she acknowledged that her fears were based on her feelings. The client admitted she always had a tendency to engage in negative what-ifs. This clinician pointed out to her that those what-ifs were not facts but assumptions and conjectures. I suggested that she stuck with the facts as she knew them to be at the time. If the facts changed, she would deal with the new reality. I acknowledged that ceasing to engage in those negative what-ifs would be a process. But over time, as she eventually caught herself engaging in feelings vs. facts, she would let facts dictate an appropriate response.

I found this quote (author unknown) very beneficial to offer clients: "Anxiety is the refusal to accept things in life the way they are, rather than the way you want them to be. If we can learn to accept life on life's terms, we can substantially lower our own anxiety." So, the first step for the client in reducing their anxiety is to notice it and bring it to their consciousness. Then, the next step is to acknowledge how little control they have over the situation that makes them anxious, such as being in rush-hour traffic. I don't know how recent a saying has become, but I often use it with clients when they report negative self-talk or negative what-ifs that create their anxiety, "And how is that working for you?" So, when we can't control what is happening, we can control how we react to a situation.

I found this list of things we can control ("Things We Can Control: Treats For The Soul, March 22, 2022, by Medard Laz) that I want to include in this discussion: "our beliefs, attitudes, perspective, how honest we are, who our friends are, what books we read, how often we exercise, the types of foods we eat, how many risks we take, how kind you are to others and yourself, how often you say I love you and thank you. In addition, there are other things we can control, which include how you express your feelings if you are able to ask for help, how often you acknowledge gratitude, how many times you smile in a day, the amount of effort you put forth, how you spend and invest your money, how much time you spend worrying, how much time you spend thinking about the past, whether or not you judge other people (including yourself), whether or not you try after a setback, and how much you appreciate the things you have." How different would our lives be if we sought to implement these recommendations?

Would a discussion on anxiety be complete if we didn't include how stress can affect our sleep? For us to be able to fall and stay asleep, our minds have to be blank, like an erased blackboard. I tell clients that the bed is where we sleep, not trying to solve our or the world's problems. It also helps the bedroom to be cool, not overly warm, and with minimal light (not more than a night light). If you have to get out of bed to get a drink of water or go to the bathroom, do not turn on any lights, but have your home set up with nightlights. When trying to sleep, turning on lights severs the melatonin in our brain and makes it harder to fall back asleep. It would also make sense not to look at our cell phones or look at an actual clock when we are trying to sleep. A good suggestion regarding the cell phone would be to leave it in another room or turn it off altogether.

Regarding a clock, put a piece of cardboard or turn it away so you will not be tempted to look at it in the middle of the night. Looking at the clock while trying to sleep is an anxiety provoker. Another suggestion is to listen to non-vocal music beside your bed and perhaps use relaxation techniques (deep breathing, imagery, progressive muscle tensing, and relaxation). If you can't fall asleep or you have awakened and can't fall back asleep, stay in bed anyway. At least you are resting (being inactive), and resting has to be better than getting out of bed and being active.

Before going to bed, ask yourself if there is a stressor that can keep you from falling asleep or could wake you up in the middle of the night. If the answer is yes, then write the stressor on paper outside the bedroom. Also, write down possible strategies that you will implement the next day. Your strategies become your Plan of Action. And establishing a plan is better than having no plan. And having a plan may help you fall and stay asleep as long as you keep the stressor and your plan of action outside your bedroom.

Another recommendation you can use with your clients is to help them with their anxiety. Imagine they bring an imaginary knapsack into the counseling session. In the knapsack are their stressors that resemble rocks or small boulders. You could ask them how heavy the knapsack they were carrying. Maybe you could encourage them to discard the heavy contents (those stressors) and only keep the "gold nuggets." The gold nuggets are symbolic of strategies or lessons learned. Therefore, only those nuggets are worth carrying.

Substance Abuse

"I can stop anytime." "I like the way it makes me feel." "I drink or use the drug to help me relax, to help me be more sociable, or give me more confidence." These are the statements uttered by previous clients. I want to share an example of a recent client with you.

7-4 A Female Client & Her Substance Abuse

During the intake, this female client admitted that she uses alcohol, occasionally mushrooms, and even men to fill a void; substances help her be an extrovert. In addition, she realized that bad things have happened to her when under the influence of alcohol or her drug of choice (such as having a one-night stand with her boyfriend's best friend and, another time, breaking bones in her foot). She said she doesn't drink or use mushrooms when she is by herself; it is always with friends. She admitted to consuming 7-12 bottles of alcohol a week, and tequila is her alcohol of choice. She was resistant to attending an alcohol or substance abuse group. When she indulges, I asked whether it is alcohol or a drug and who controls whom. Can she control her consumption or drug use, or do they control her? Has she ever told herself that she would only consume a certain quantity and not exceed that amount when she drinks? Her answer was "no." She has never been able to limit the number of drinks she has consumed on any occasion. After several sessions, she finally conceded that her consumption was controlling her, and she admitted that she believed she needed more than counseling or a support group. She found a facility in California and arranged to enter their program independently. Counseling resumed after her discharge, and she has remained abstinent from all substances.

Working with clients with substance abuse issues is difficult because they are in denial that their abuse is causing problems in their life. You have heard the expression of clients hitting rock bottom. For many, hitting bottom might mean they have lost their marriage, job, residence, or all of the above because they would not admit that their substance abuse had become more important to them than anything else. We have learned not to force clients to acknowledge that they are an alcoholic or a substance abuser. For me, I resist the temptation to label them an alcoholic. Instead, an effective clinician will continue to ask these clients questions, thereby helping them to realize that their inability to control their alcohol consumption or their substance use has taken over their lives.

An effective technique to use with these populations is Motivation Interviewing. Motivational Interviewing is a collaborative, client-centered psychotherapeutic approach that attempts to help clients explore and overcome ambivalence about changing negative behaviors. It is the therapist's role to help clients believe that change is possible and that they are capable of achieving it. In addition, it encourages patients to think and talk about their reasons for reducing or quitting a substance (Miller & Rollnick).

The clinician employs the use of asking the client a lot of open-ended questions. The therapist spends a great deal of time listening, repeating what the client has shared, and attempting to see the situation from the client's perspective without being judgmental. While using this technique, clinicians focus on expressing empathy with the client, helping the client address the discrepancy their substance use is causing in their lives.

The therapist employs the use of (OARS): Open-ended questions, Affirmations, Reflective listening, and Summaries to help guide the client toward the change and goals they want to accomplish (Miller & Rollnick). An example of an open-ended question is, "What has worked for you in the past when you made a difficult change?" Affirmations are a great way to highlight the client's strengths when they can only recognize their weaknesses and failures. Reflective listening is a communication strategy that seeks to understand a client's idea and then offer the view back to the client to confirm that the concept has been understood correctly. Reflective listening is more strategic than just actively listening. Finally, summaries are a special kind of reflective listening in which the clinician takes the information shared by the client and provides an opportunity to deliver the data back to the client more coherently. Then, the clinician can ask them to consider what that means to them.

In using Motivational Interviewing, the psychotherapist avoids getting into arguments with the client over their abuse. And whatever resistance the client is putting up, the clinician "rolls with the resistance." When resistance occurs, the clinician helps the client to consider changing their strategy. The emphasis is to ensure that the patients actively participate in this process. This technique empowers clients and allows them to explore how to make a difference in their health and well-being while drawing attention to past successes and eliciting strengths, not weaknesses. This model works best when these clients have mixed feelings about changing their behavior. The Motivational Interviewing counselor needs to be formally trained and experienced and should employ the skills of being empathetic and a good listener. In addition to substance abuse, Motivational Interviewing can be used with cigarette smoking, compulsive gambling, sex addiction, internet gaming addiction, and eating disorders. In addition, Motivational Interviewing can be used with Cognitive Behavioral. This approach has helped many people who struggle with addiction. It addresses their motivation and helps get them on a healthy path. While it is beneficial to many clients, it is not a treatment course for all patients with substance use disorders. Every individual needs to be assessed to determine the type of therapy that will work for them. If you are further interested in Motivational Interviewing, I highly encourage you to seek out a book specifically on this topic.

7-5 Another Challenging Alcohol Abuser

Recently, I was counseling a married couple with the following facts. The couple consisted of the husband, 38 years old, and his wife, 37. They have been married for 17 years, and they have a son who is 14 years old and a 13-year-old daughter. During the intake, it was revealed that the husband had been abusing alcohol throughout their marriage. He admitted that his choice of beverage is beer and that his typical consumption is over 12 beers whenever he is out with friends, with the goal of being intoxicated. He and his friends will often drink at one of his friends' homes. His wife had always told him that she would prefer him to be sober enough to drive home without incident, and if that is not possible, then he should spend the night at his friend's home. He interpreted what his wife said as having her blessings not to come home if he abused alcohol.

As I began to counsel this couple, I decided not to dwell exclusively on the husband's alcohol abuse but also to focus on strengthening their communication skills and helping them find common interests in their marriage. However, I was met with resistance each time I attempted to inquire about the husband's alcohol consumption. Finally, he was able to admit that in the past, he had stopped drinking for a while when he believed his drinking was becoming "out of control." Unfortunately, these periods did not last long, and he admitted that he quickly returned to the same quantity that prompted his decision to stop.

During the course of counseling them, I tried several techniques with him, and they included Motivational Interviewing. I posed questions to him, such as the benefits of his drinking and the quantity of his consumption. I also asked if he is able to control his consumption when he drinks or if it controls him, and if he would be open to considering reducing his consumption to what he could consume and still drive home again without incident. Finally, I reminded him and his wife that they are role models for their children. So, what education would they offer their children about alcohol and drinking responsibly, and is the husband a good role model? After posing these questions at each subsequent session, I asked the husband to respond while also improving their communication and helping them establish common interests they can share together.

At the end of one session, the husband left abruptly, stating that he believed I was siding with his wife. He thought his wife and I were accusing him of being a "bad father" when he chose to drink and either spend the night at a friend's house or sleep in his car outside the bar once he had become intoxicated.

The husband opted not to accompany his wife in the next session, so the wife was seen individually. During that session, the wife revealed that her husband admitted that he knows his drinking is out of control and that his drinking needs to be addressed, but he felt we were ganging up on him in marital sessions. I reached out to him, and he agreed that I would see him individually to focus on this alcohol abuse. He was agreeable to continue marital counseling so long as the sessions focused again on issues such as communication, bonding exercises, and helping them resolve some of their other stressors.

Editorial comment: A counselor must be adaptable and flexible when a client has become defensive or needs to change how sessions are conducted. I have often said, particularly in marital counseling, that I will provide couples counseling so long as no issue, such as substance abuse, prevents us from success. If this occurred, I would suggest that I meet individually with the alcohol abuser, which may indicate that marital counseling may need to be put on the back burner.

And that is precisely what happened. I recognized that, at present, it did not seem possible for me to see the couple for marital counseling without offering individual counseling to the husband, addressing his issues, and perhaps focusing on why he tends to abuse alcohol. When I suggested this proposal to the husband, he said he was not ready to meet individually. I believe sometime in the future, the husband will contact me when he is able to admit again that his drinking is out of control and/or his wife perhaps has given him an ultimatum.

Someone once provided me with these insights: Be careful when you want more for your clients than they want for themselves. For example, clients may stop counseling because they are not ready to deal with an issue and for the therapist not to take their decision personally. The individual may seek therapy later on, perhaps when the issue is affecting them more intensely or if their partner is threatening them with an ultimatum.

Schizophrenics

Throughout my career, I have not encountered very many schizophrenics, either in my employment or in my private practice. I know they are a challenge to every clinician, mainly because, like bipolar clients, it is difficult to convince people with schizophrenia to remain on their medication. Either they do not like the way they feel while on the medication, or they do not believe they need the medication at all. The following is the experience I had with my first schizophrenic client when I was a new intake counselor in my first mental health job.

7-6 My First Schizophrenic Client

Before seeing this intake, our receptionist informed me that the individual was experiencing delusions. As I was escorting him to my office, I didn't have a clue what I was going to say or how I was going to help him. I began this intake as I always have, "What brought you in today? How can I be of assistance to you." He replied, "I have a transmitter that was installed in my head, and I want it removed." I decided to treat him as I would any other intake. I began asking him follow-up questions, such as when the transmitter was installed, why it is a problem for him now, and many more inquiries. Again, as a clinician, you never want to challenge them and try to convince them that their delusion is all in their head (pardon the pun). As I continued to question him, at the same time, I wondered how I was going to help him. At the end of the intake, I offered the following recommendation, "You said you want the transmitter removed, and I can refer you to a hospital where they can remove it. And the good news is that surgery will not have to be performed. Medication can be prescribed, which will continuously shrink the transmitter and make it go away." He was very pleased with the referral, and he went into the psychiatric hospital willingly.

I want to share another case with you with the following client:

7-7 A Client's Son

I was providing counseling to a female client, and in between sessions, she called and asked if her son could accompany her to her next appointment. Of course, I said sure. So, on the next visit, I met with the client and her son. The mother informed me that her son was a freshman in college and had difficulty managing his stress. I began asking the son questions about the origin of his anxiety, and that was when he admitted that he believed that others could read his mind. His delusions were so consuming that they prevented him from concentrating on his courses. I noticed the mother was very shaken at her son's admission in my peripheral vision. So, I took charge. I suggested that I could assist them in getting the son evaluated by a psychiatrist for a medication that could help him with his "stress" (delusions). I assured them that the doctor could write a letter to the university asking for a medical leave for the rest of the semester. I also suggested that he should agree to individual counseling and that he take any medication that would be prescribed. Both were pleased with my recommendation. I resumed seeing the mother achieve her goals, and I was able to obtain progress reports on her son. Once on medication and regularly seeing a therapist, he returned to school the next semester and was doing well.

Again, these two cases exemplify the importance of asking questions, remaining non-judgmental, and not challenging clients about their beliefs in their delusions or hallucinations. Instead, clinicians offer a solution that the client will hopefully accept. I equate the process of asking them questions and searching for answers is similar to playing checkers, chess, or billiards. First, I anticipate what their replies will be to my questions and decide what my next "moves" will be (my responses). Then, I may summarize the client's words and offer an opinion, conclusion, or hypothesis. It is okay if the client replies that your conclusions or hypotheses were incorrect. If this were to happen, the clinician would offer their apology and ask the client to kindly clarify what the counselor missed. Then again, the therapist would attempt to summarize what the client has disseminated.

Don't allow any client's presenting issues to intimidate you. After you complete the intake, you can always refer them to a colleague if you don't feel comfortable counseling a client after they reveal their issues or the presenting problems are beyond your training. One of the benefits of being in private practice is choosing the clients we want to assist. I also remember the advice of previous supervisors to always stay in our lanes, which would include within our training and what is being asked of us, perhaps by the client or a managed care company, if you are under contract.

CHAPTER 8:

Current Topics In The News That Needed To Be Addressed

I DEBATED WHETHER to include these additional topics and how I would address them in this book. I haven't forgotten that this book's central premise is about helping future clinicians be the best they can be. I probably would not have added these issues if I had not taken the class on Cultural Diversity, which I will describe below. However, I want to include issues therapists may and probably will encounter with their clients and colleagues. Our profession seems to have been hijacked by radical ideology, and those who are thrusting this ideology are attempting to force therapists to accept where they want to take the profession. Unfortunately, it appears that the following subjects have injected themselves into today's society like the tentacles of an octopus, and they may continue to surface more often. If the therapist does not accept and adopt their philosophies, they may be subject to ridicule and become ostracized. So, I want to offer my readers and colleagues alternate views on dealing with these issues when they are encountered in counseling sessions with clients and when dealing with colleagues in public.

Cultural Diversity and Microaggressions

While employed at the Federal EAP, I was asked to become licensed in another state (I won't name that state). When I sent my application to the state for licensure, the licensing board replied that they could not find Cultural Diversity on my transcript. When I obtained my graduate degree in 1980, this course was not considered to be taught. My employer suggested I find a university to take the course and submit evidence that I had completed and passed the class. So, I found a university and enrolled in this "Multicultural Counseling" class in 2011. So here I was in my mid-50s, taking a graduate course. As you can imagine, I was the oldest student in the class. I went into the class open-minded until I began reading the textbook. I don't think I have disagreed more with a textbook than this one! Consequently, I announced to the instructor and the students (in a very diplomatic way), that I would be the antagonist in the class. I shared with the students and the professor that I had been successfully providing therapy to clients long before I was exposed to a cultural diversity class and textbook.

The author, Jerry Diller, stated that cross-cultural counseling is "more demanding, challenging and energy demanding than work with same cultural clients." Furthermore, he emphasizes that one cannot be an effective therapist unless one changes how one conducts therapy to accommodate each client's race and culture. The author contends that "standard approaches are overwhelmingly culture-bound and Northern European in nature." However, the book fails to reveal an approach that would not effectively work with minority cultures. Furthermore, it fails to offer strategies that should be used with each culture or all minority cultures. In an earlier chapter of this book, I mentioned that the first thing we learned in graduate school is the importance of building a rapport with our clients. Again, I do two things with every client: ask them what goals they want to accomplish in therapy, and at the end of each session, I ask if I am meeting their needs and whether counseling is moving toward achieving their goals. Culture does have a place as a therapist conduct their sessions. I will, for instance, ask a married couple who are from a different culture to educate me about their culture and traditions. When I decide on techniques (many of them were presented in the earlier chapters) to use with clients/couples, I pick ones that can be utilized based on their presenting issues. The techniques I employ can be used with every culture or race. Then my second goal is to successfully establish a rapport with every client, couple, or family. Again, I want the best for everyone who comes through my office door, and I want to help them achieve their counseling goals.

The author was very comfortable with counselors advocating on their clients' behalf to seek "social justice" in cases where discrimination, racism, etc., have occurred. However, clinicians must be cautious when considering being directly involved in seeking social justice for their clients when signing contracts with managed care and insurance companies. They could violate their agreement if they encourage their clients to pursue social justice at their workplace or if the clinician is considering advising the client to hire an attorney and taking their company to court. That also means that a therapist must recognize that insurance and managed care companies have a dual relationship, and they cannot encourage the client to take their case to the Equal Employment Opportunity Commission (EEOC),

That doesn't mean a therapist cannot suggest to their clients not to speak up or take action if their grievances are with their supervisor or the company where they are employed, but their actions must be within the workplace. The employee/client can take their complaint to their Human Resources Dept and must become familiar with the company's policies and procedures. However, before recommending that, the employee can attempt to work out their issues with their supervisor. If I were their therapist, I would offer the client a script to use with their manager or HR Dept. If a client receives counseling through their insurance or EAP and states they are considering hiring an attorney or taking their situation to EEOC; I would not dissuade them. That is their purgative; I just cannot plant the seed or recommend an action beyond what is permitted within the company.

The textbook's author on Cultural Diversity could have recommended how therapists could conduct counseling with differing cultures. But, no, the author spent pages and chapters bringing up subjects that will not unite us together as therapists or as a country. For example, in this course about cultural diversity, it irked me to see concepts such as "white privilege," "white supremacy," and "white guilt" presented and accepted by university administrators and professors in a graduate school course. Again, I don't know how these concepts help us in the mental health field, our country, or as a society. I had been counseling clients of different races and cultures for almost 30 years before I enrolled in this class. I believe (often verified by clients) that I seek to be as color-blind a therapist as possible. I hope that sometime in the future, as cultural diversity courses are offered, they do not attempt to make the white therapist feel guilty about their race, a race that was not of their choosing. Instead, as these courses continue, it is my hope that it helps therapists succeed with all their clients by emphasizing our similarities, not our differences. And acknowledging that clients want to lead happy and productive lives and they desire tools to help their relationship thrive, and this is true for all races and cultures. I believe these are the roles of a therapist.

The textbook on Cultural Diversity also spent a good deal of space in one of his chapters, espousing racial microaggressions. In a Ted Talk by Tiffany Alvoid entitled, "Eliminating Microaggressions: The Next Level," racial Microaggression has been defined as a term used for "brief and commonplace daily verbal, behavioral, or environmental indignities, whether intentional or unintentional, that communicate hostile, derogatory, or negative prejudicial slights and insults toward any group." He assumed that just because a clinician is white, they would automatically engage in microaggressions in therapy sessions. He also stated that whites view themselves as good, moral, and decent. I aspire to those attributes, which I think are true of all my clients and colleagues. And I treat all my clients with respect and dignity.

Chapter 8-1 Example of A Cultural Diversity Case

So, let me offer a real counseling case as one of many examples of how I have successfully worked with a client and couples of a different culture than me. As with other clients, I was able to establish a great rapport, this time with a married Hispanic female. She continued to schedule appointments because of our ability to address and discuss strategies for her many presenting issues. When she initially made an intake appointment, she complained about her husband and marriage. After meeting with her for a few sessions, with my encouragement, she got her husband to agree to accompany her to a few sessions. While talking with the couple to discuss both the marriage and them as individuals, I got the husband to admit that he was not taking care of his health. He acknowledged that being overweight probably led him to first being diagnosed as pre-diabetic and then as a diabetic. His abuse of alcohol was also not helpful to his condition, including his marriage. In counseling them as a couple, I tried to balance helping them improve the quality of their marriage and encouraging the husband to take better care of himself. However, the husband may have stopped coming to the sessions because the focus was on him for his part in not contributing to a happier relationship and his inability to commit to better health.

Even though the husband refused to participate in further sessions, the wife continued. She stated that her husband continues to abuse alcohol and even has their children in his vehicle while drinking. In addition, he has taken no action to lose weight or to take steps to control his diabetes. She said she never saw how her husband had been influenced by his parents and the Machismo culture. The wife, my client, has told him the things she would like them to do as a couple, such as dancing, and he refuses to not only participate with her but wants to forbid her from taking dance lessons with men. She said he has made derogatory comments referring to her as "his woman" as though she is his possession.

As I write this book, I continue to see this client. She stated she is not sure she wants to remain married if her husband refuses to take steps to the changes she would require of him. I suggested that she begin a list of non-negotiable changes she would require of him, give him a reasonable time limit, and she would consider separating from him if he did not implement those changes. In the meantime, it was agreed that she would open her own savings account and explore alternative living arrangements for herself and her children. As a marriage and family therapist, my role is not to advocate that she divorce or even separate from her husband but for the wife to convince him that she is reaching her limit and that the husband needs to decide if the marriage and family are worth fighting for.

There is an area where I agree with the author on Cultural Diversity, and that is to be aware that different cultures and races may have different mores in their marriage or upbringing. From this case example, I needed to know about the Machismo within the Hispanic culture to ascertain if she was raised to accept this in her marriage or if she rebelled from this perhaps past cultural belief.

Critical Race Theory

Critical Race Theory (CRT) originated from the European Marxist School of critical theory. Critical race theory is an academic movement that seeks to establish a link between racism, race, and power. Critical Race Theory is not like the Civil Rights movement, where the goal was to work within America's democracy. Instead, critical race theorists challenge liberal order, such as rationalism, constitutional law, and legal reasoning. Instead, these race theorists argue that American social life, political structures, and economic systems are founded upon race. And racism is seen in virtually every facet of society.

So, the folks behind this movement say they want to make the admissions processes in colleges and universities more equitable. For example, they would consider eliminating standard tests and perhaps adding a diversity/equity score to applications. In addition, they would require students and faculty to understand their (assumed) biases and racism by forcing them to receive training or classes. Again, taking a Cultural Diversity Class was required of me, and I believe currently, every student at most public universities or colleges is required to take a similar course. The faculty would also emphasize anti-racist ideology in their classes and material. Some books on anti-racism would be required reading. On campuses, they have clamped down on freedom of speech and academic freedoms by revising codes of conduct and implementing vague language on what is perceived as "hate speech" and "racist language." There is no tolerance for students or faculty who do not subscribe to this movement. With virtually no discussion, there has been a push to rename buildings and schools. Some statues are being torn down while buildings and schools are being renamed. Some prominent names such as Thomas Jefferson, Robert E. Lee, and Ulysses Grant are included because they were once slave owners or were affiliated with the Confederacy during the Civil War. I believe preserving our history, even history that makes us uncomfortable, is vital. We cannot learn from history if it is no longer taught, as it helps us to avoid repeating past mistakes.

I want to offer this past client whom I once saw as an example of counseling a client from a different culture. A male client requested counseling, stating he had recently moved to the mainland of the US from Puerto Rico. He complained that neither his coworkers nor his employer were culturally accommodating him as a Puerto Rican. I used the following analogy with him. After Hurricane Katrina flooded a considerable part of New Orleans' population decided to move out of the city, and many settled in the Dallas/Fort Worth area. Some say that folks from New Orleans have a specific culture, but they would have to assimilate when they moved away. I suggested to this client that rather than expecting others to accommodate him, they expected him to assimilate into his new environment. He could share his culture with his workplace- perhaps they might be sensitive to his challenges. My challenge was "planting a seed" to get him to understand that he was not in Puerto Rico anymore, as were the folks who had moved from New Orleans. So, in counseling him, I focused on his feeling of being alienated and not feeling he belonged. In time, through the suggestions I offered, he took steps to assimilate, finding those common interests he shared with coworkers and others with whom he eventually became friends.

Wokeism

The term has been defined as being "alert to racial prejudice and discrimination." I believe most individuals could accept this definition. However, here are some examples of the positions of folks who embrace being woked and opposing views. Woke promotes social justice and equality. However, equality is not what is sought; instead, what is desired is equity. Again, equity is changing the rules or even laws so individuals or groups can achieve a specific desired outcome. Often, to achieve equity, someone or a group of people are discriminated against or passed over so that equity and equality can occur. Woke actively attempts to silence views that are in dispute with the cancel culture. Those who agree with Woke state that the goal is to make people who are minorities feel more comfortable and noticed. Those who oppose woke observe that proponents of woke see virtually everything through the lens of racial identity.

Wokeism's core belief is that America is a deplorable, irredeemable nation that is rooted in racism, sexism, and imperialism. Students are taught to feel responsibility, guilt, or anguish for what other race members did in the past. Also, students who are taught wokeism in high school and colleges would embrace the 1619 Project, where it is emphasized that the United States was founded on slavery. The 1619 Project was initiated in August 2019 to acknowledge the 400th anniversary of the first enslaved Africans arriving in colonial Virginia. However, the first enslaved Africans were actually brought to North America in 1526. Those who believe in wokesim and the 1619 Project state that the only way the US can redeem itself is through continued reverse discrimination and racism. Some continue to push for reparations, where the US would give decedents of former slaves a monetary sum. The goal of wokeism is to do away with our current system by declaring that the Declaration of Independence principles were again based on racism and slavery and should be replaced with a plan that seeks social justice.

In 2022, check out this headline, "Is Math Racist?" Jason Rantz wrote an opinion article for Newsweek entitled," 'Math is Racist' Crowd Runs Rampant in Seattle, Portland." He stated, "The basic argument from the "math is racist" crowd is that "white supremacy culture" is endemic to mathematics classrooms, and it's why black students' math scores are lagging white students." In addition, some asserted that objective mathematics is rooted in "white supremacist patriarchy" and white social constructs. Finally, some ask if math is racist because the concepts originated from whites from Western culture.

In addition, consider this headline from 2022: "Study Examines Whiteness in Physics, Finds Whiteboards Are Racist," by M. Dowling from the Independent Sentinel from March 22, 2022. Those that believe this state, "meritocracies and whiteboards are whiteness and whites are racist. Whiteness is white supremacy, and physics has the demography it has because of white supremacy."

As you can see, these beliefs have gone from the classroom to parts of our society and culture. And if these viewpoints are challenged, the challengers are called racists. Wokeism leads local, state, and federal governments to pick and choose which laws are enforced or not, including parts of the First Amendment, including Freedom of

Speech, Freedom to Assemble, etc. The adoption of these concepts has led to an acceptance of systemic and institutional racism, unconscious bias, white privilege, and white fragility. Companies, corporations, and even the federal government have been bullied and shamed into providing trainings on such topics as cultural diversity that are taught by social justice activists. The accepted definition of "woke" is to be alert or woken up, be aware of any prejudice and discrimination, be opposed to any, and seek remedy when it occurs in any form. I certainly can accept this definition, but not if the remedy is to punish any race or culture for the treatment of another in the past. That is as wrong as what happened in the past, from Blacks who were enslaved during the colonial period to the Japanese as US citizens who were interned during World War II and the treatment of the American Indians (to offer such a few examples). In the future, in this century and beyond, we must embrace equality for all (without punishing any culture or race) and ensure all can pursue the American dream and all rights reserved in the Constitution.

Despite my hope to achieve these goals in the future, it will continue to be a challenge. As I continued to write this book, students who will graduate in 2026 from a medical school in Minnesota were requested to pledge, "We commit to uprooting the legacy and perpetuation of the structural violence deeply embedded within the healthcare system. We recognize inequity built by past and current traumas rooted in white supremacy, colonialism, gender binary, ableism, and all forms of oppression. As we enter into this profession with growth and opportunity for promoting a culture of anti-racism, listening and amplifying voices for positive change."

Dr. Mark McDonald, a child and adolescent psychiatrist practicing in Los Angeles, CA, and also has his podcast, has a more promising prediction. He believes diversity, equity, and inclusion (DEI) is the beginning of the end for medical care in the US. He states that, currently, ideology has been included in almost every facet of healthcare. However, he believes DEI could lead those in the medical field to break away from the liberal wing of the profession and could lead to an alternative to how medical students are trained. In addition, it could lead to repudiation from DEI, CRT, and Wokeism. He further said that in the long run, this alternative to the liberal bent in the medical field might make medical care less expensive, more accessible, more affordable, and ethical.

I am also encouraged by the comments of Adam B. Coleman, author of "Black Victim to Black Victor." He took a psychological perspective in describing someone who is a survivor of trauma. He said we wouldn't tell the survivor to constantly relive the trauma and to constantly harbor that resentment. If they were to continue to relive the trauma and harbor the resentment, they wouldn't be able to grow or move forward. He stated that regarding past treatments of blacks in this country, blacks should not forget, but they shouldn't dwell on it either. He further asserted that current blacks in this country did not experience slavery, and none of the current population in the US were slave owners. He concluded that we, as a nation, need to acknowledge that we have more in common with each other than our differences. So, in summary, it is essential to emphasize that those who want us to accept DEI are advocating divisiveness over acceptance.

Androgyny, Non-Binary And Transgenderism:

Despite what some experts would have you believe, there are some similarities between androgyny and non-binary. For example, the Merriam-Webster dictionary defines androgyny as 1: having the characteristics or nature of both male and female androgynous heroines; 2a: neither specifically feminine nor masculine. b: suitable to or for either sex; 3: having traditional male and female roles obscured or reversed, such as an androgynous marriage.

However, Jean Perea, in her article on August 26, 2021, "Why androgyny and Non-Binary Are Not The Same Thing." She states, "Let's talk about being non-binary (again) and the difference between that and being androgynous. In short, non-binary (or genderqueer, or whatever other gender you might go by, including 'man' or 'woman') is what you identify with in your head. Whereas masculine, feminine, and androgynous are all adjectives used to describe how someone physically looks (but as noted, Merriam-Webster broadened the definition to include more than how someone physically looks). She continues, "Since gender is something you personally identify within your head, non-binary is a gender. Sex, on the other hand, is what's between your legs. The terms we use for that are male, female, and intersex." She includes the definition from the World Health Organization (WHO), "Gender refers to the characteristics of women, men, girls, and boys that are socially constructed. This includes norms, behaviours, and roles associated with being a woman, man, girl, or boy, as well as relationships with each other. As a social construct, gender varies from society to society and can change over time."

Dr. Miriam Grossman is a child, adolescent, and adult psychiatrist and an author. Her most recent book is entitled, "Lost In Trans Nation: A Child Psychiatrist's Guide Out Of The Madness." On June 23, 2023, she testified before the House Committee On Energy and Commerce. She said one's sex and gender are not assigned at birth, but instead, they are established at conception and recognized at birth. To believe they are assigned at birth is without any scientific evidence. She asserted, "Its language misleads people, especially children, into thinking that male and female are arbitrary designations and can change. That is simply not true."

Dr. Jordan Peterson, Ph.D., a professor of psychology at the University of Toronto, believes the gender identity movement is anti-scientific at its foundation. As a society, we are being ordered to change our thinking and institutions. And if we do not alter our thinking and accept this movement, we risk being ostracized or worse. Dr. Peterson explained how breaking these stereotypes of being male or female doesn't make one a transgender person. Dr. Peterson said in an article in the Daily Wire by Amanda Prestigiacomo on January 26, 2022, entitled "Jordan Peterson Talks Gender Ideology, "We have this idea in our culture that you can be a woman born in a man's body, And that's not true. But you can definitely be a man with a feminine personality structure. When men are feminine or women are masculine, that doesn't mean they're in the wrong body. It just means that men and women are more alike than different." He asserted that gender identity is based on personality differences and is not biology-based. He said he could accept that people are "gender fluid." He offered the example of a male with feminine stereotypes. Here are some feminine vs. male stereotypes. Females tend to be passive while men are active; women are more talkative than men; women tend to be more sensitive to others while men are less so; women are more emotional, while men are stereotypically more logical. Women are more verbal, while men are more analytical; women tend to be more diplomatic, men are blunter, and women are more nurturing. Dr. Peterson said Mick Jagger and David Bowie are two examples of men who do not fit into the typical male stereotypes. He stated that the same could be said of females, who display masculine traits or stereotypes. He concluded that non-binary gender identity is not rooted in biology; it is a product of a societal construct.

So, let's bring biology into the discussion. The following came from a video at Prager University, and the speaker was Colin Wright, who has a Ph.D. in Evolutionary Biology and is a Fellow at Manhattan Institute. He states that one's sex is either male or female; they are binary and immutable, meaning one's sex cannot be changed. He reminded folks of the biology in play, where male sperm fertilizes a female egg in the ovary. The fetus will either be male or female; there is no other sex. A small percentage of individuals are born with both male and female sex organs or other sexual characteristics. The biological term for this phenomenon is intersex. Intersex and transgender are not the same at all. Dr. Wright states that intersex is a rare condition resulting in apparent sex ambiguity. Transgender are not sex ambiguous at all. They all claim to identify as something different from their biological sex.

Dr. Wright said some people contend that one's sex is on a continuum. Some believe classifying sex as only males and females is outdated and should be abandoned. They want society to embrace the term "gender identity" instead. For example, men should not be barred from women's sports or women's bathrooms as long as they identify as female. He is emphatic that transwomen are unambiguous males, so the chances of a doctor inadvertently recording their sex incorrectly is zero.

Dr. Wright states the transgender policy in sports and in society is that the individual's sex needs to correspond to the sex on the birth certificate. If there isn't a birth certificate to refer to, then the decision is based on one's biology, not on the individual's feelings. His final quote is: "One can identify as anything they would like, but one's identity does not determine biological reality. The reality is sex in humans is immutable and binary.

There is one more point that Dr. Wright made, as illustrated in the graph below. Some believe that there has been a surge in those individuals born with ambiguous genitalia. Instead, he contends there has been an increase in individuals claiming to identify as the opposite sex from the one in which they were born.

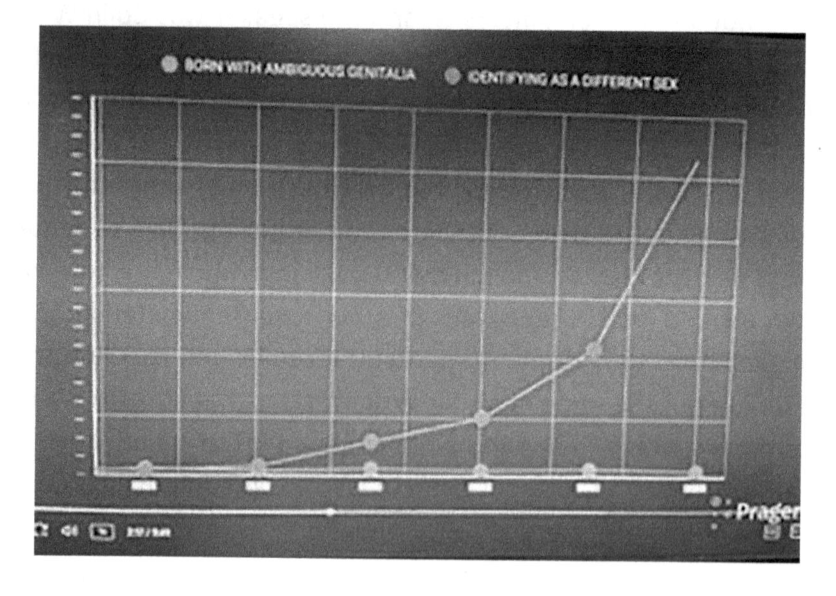

In the graph above, the line at the bottom of the graph signifies those born with ambiguous genitalia (both male and female sex organs and other sexual characteristics). The advancing line indicates the increase in the number of individuals identifying as a different sex.

So, let's return to Dr. Jordan Peterson. In the interview conducted by Ben Shapiro, Dr. Jordan Peterson also elaborated on his view of psychotherapy and those with gender identity issues by saying, "Therapy helps people sort out their problems." He said therapists should not be "rubber stampers" as it occurs in affirmation therapy, where the therapist just agrees with the client regarding their gender identity. Dr. Peterson stated this is not therapy. Instead, a good therapist will help clients process their thoughts and behaviors. More often than not, the client is coming to counseling because of their struggle over their gender identity. Perhaps, they would not have questioned their gender identity if it were not due in part, to how liberal our society has become.

Can A Man Become Pregnant? Yes, writes KC Clements from the article by the same title, "Can Men Become Pregnant," from Healthline on December 20, 2018. He wrote, "Yes, it's possible for men to become pregnant and give birth to children of their own. In fact, it's a lot more common than you might think. In order to explain, we'll need to break down some common misconceptions about how we understand the term "man." Not all people who were assigned male at birth identify as men." Hence, this is the problem with this article and what folks like him want us to believe and accept. In this viewpoint, we as a society will have to accept the changing of the term "male." The belief is not to accept the gender we were born with but the gender we are assigned or what gender we want to accept. These notions are in contrast with biology. Men, biologically speaking, cannot get pregnant because they do not have a uterus or ovaries. It is all about changing the definitions of terms that have been accepted since dictionaries defined them. All these beliefs are designed to confuse us and complicate the issues, as does the next topic.

The Use of Transgender Pronouns

Here is a story that occurred when this book was written, and it is a concern of things to come. Here is the story. In the spring of 2022, three male 8th graders were allegedly charged with sexual harassment for not using proper pronouns. The school district was enforcing its ability to police student speech. It added that the students were subjected to yelling and name-calling for refusing to use non-biological pronouns, even as administrators failed to use their preferred pronouns. I believe we will continue to see stories like this that will impact our society until we make our voices heard, that our voice is the majority, and we will not allow others to control our freedom of speech.

So, let me provide you with what I believe are facts. There is the belief that there are still only two genders, male and female, which has been accepted throughout our existence, despite what some would have you believe. For those who think otherwise, permit me to share this argument: it is the mind that has made an individual uncomfortable with the sex/gender they were born with. It is all about what a person identifies with, including transgender, non-binary, or gender-neutral. The person identifies who they are currently, but their identity can change over time.

This has led to these individuals requiring society to change to the non-gendered, non-binary pronouns that are not gender-specific such as "ze" in place of she/he and "hir" in place of his/him/her. In addition, individuals who identify as not entirely male or female will often use gender-neutral pronouns, such as "they" or "them." This is quite confusing because "they" and "them" are typically used as plurals. These individuals want to believe they have the right to use their selected pronouns that match their personal identity, but they also want to force all of us to use them. To further complicate the matter, their personal identity and pronouns may not match their gender expression, such as how they dress, look, behave, or the name they use. All of these identities are created in one's mind, and it was their biological gender that occurred first. I don't want to discount people struggling with sexuality and gender. I know it is a genuine struggle, and I have had an abundance of clients to prove it. My point is that these individuals can ask us for our empathy and equality without requiring us to change our use of language as it relates to transgender pronouns.

All these views: white guilt, white privilege, white supremacy, CRT, Wokeism, and forcing society into using transgender pronouns only pit races and cultures against each other. They fuel hate and can encourage violence when their idea of social justice does not yield the results they seek. In counseling sessions, I want to be a role model for my clients, that a white, heterosexual therapist can counsel clients of different races and cultures and help them accomplish their goals. I believe we, as counselors, should not tolerate any discrimination, including reverse discrimination. We are all a work in progress, and hopefully, we will continue to be introspective. As we do so, we can examine, and when noted, we can extinguish our biases and prejudices. We should continue to treat everyone, including our clients, with dignity and encourage them to be their best. We should demand better education for all students (including school choice) and promote their success based on hard work, tenacity, and motivation. Again, when applying for colleges/universities, admission folks would not and should not know the applicant's race. Therefore, acceptance into institutions of higher education would not be based on race. What a color-blind concept!

Gender-Affirming Care & Reassignment Surgeries

There is another subject within this chapter that has to be included and dealt with, and that is gender reassignment surgeries, which are essentially gender mutilation, that are occurring to minors and adults. Laurel Duggan from the Daily Caller, on August 18, 2022, wrote an article entitled, "Yes, Doctors Are Performing Sex Change Surgeries on Kids." And what she said in her article. "Boston Children's Hospital performs mastectomies on transgender minors as young as 15, and previous guidance allowed vaginoplasty to be performed on 17-year-olds, according to documents reviewed by the Daily Caller News Foundation. The hospital updated its guidance with a minimum age requirement of 18 for all "gender-affirming" genital surgeries and hysterectomies after being subject to criticism and threats related to its online promotion of sex change procedures, although it still allows mastectomies at 15."

It seems appropriate at this time to introduce the term gender dysphoria. The National Health Service (NHS) in the United Kingdom (UK) defines gender dysphoria as "a condition that causes distress and discomfort when the gender you identify with conflicts with the gender you were assigned at birth" Dr. Jay Richards, a senior research fellow at the DeVos Center, told the Daily Caller News Foundation went to state, "We know that until recently, almost all young kids with gender dysphoria reconciled with their sexed bodies after they get through puberty. The effect of 'gender affirmation' and early social transition, in contrast, is to put kids on a fast track to surgical intervention and sterilization,"

Ms. Duggan continued, "Several media outlets have downplayed the prevalence of transgender surgeries for minors amid controversy surrounding Boston Children's Hospital's gender center, but the hospital's own publicly available documents show that doctors are performing sex change surgeries on children."

The following came from an NBC article by Dawn Ennis on October 31, 2016 entitled "More US Hospitals Offering Gender-Affirming Surgeries." She stated, "A (financial) boon is underway at medical institutions from coast to coast, aimed at helping transgender Americans who suffer gender dysphoria because of the mismatch between their bodies and their gender identity. Gender-transition services and surgeries are Gender-transition services and surgeries are becoming more widely available across the nation, and more insurance companies are adding coverage to help more than one million Americans who identify as transgender."

The list of medical facilities offering gender reassignment surgery keeps growing. Here are some of those medical centers as of 2022: The Cleveland Clinic, Boston Medical Center, Oregon Health & Science University in Portland, Mount Sinai Hospital in New York, Duke Health, University of North Carolina (UHC) Health, and East Carolina University (ECU) Health and Vanderbilt Hospital in Nashville, Tennessee.

According to Ms. Sloan Rachmuth, the Founder and President of Education First Alliance North Carolina, she states that the age to start gender transitions at Duke is two years old; at UHC, it is three years of age; and at ECU, it is four years of age. She said these three facilities obtain their referrals from child psychiatrists, child psychologists, school counselors, and pediatricians. She asserts that these professionals would interpret symptoms such as children being uncomfortable in their bodies or a female admitting to being a tomboy. Other symptoms may include poor appetite, depression, and low self-esteem. And perhaps their obsession with social media and postings about male and female traits, for instance, may contribute to poor body image. These symptoms may lead some healthcare professionals or school officials to make a case for gender dysphoria, where both the young child and their parents would be treated at one of these three health centers. Ms. Rachmuth also said that the Duke Health Center employs mental health folks at as many as 150 schools in North Carolina. Even though she focused on the three health centers in North Carolina, gender-affirming care and reassignment surgeries are occurring across the country.

Ms. Rachmuth and her organization, Education First Alliance North Carolina, assert that pediatricians and other professionals in this state and across the country are strongly encouraged to follow the standards set by the World Professional Association of Transgender Health (WPATH). If they do not, they could face legal liability.

Finally, Ms. Rachmuth, on her organization's website, had a videotape and quotes from Dane R. Wicker, Ph.D., who in 2023 ran the clinic at Duke Health. Dr. Wicker stated it is crucial that children and adolescents go through "the right puberty," and there are repercussions of not going through "the wrong puberty." And some children and adolescents should not be allowed to go through the normal process of puberty. He said, "Schools are a safe environment for transgender and non-binary children." The only responsibility they have is the education of our children, not to indoctrinate them into believing that because they may be uncomfortable in their bodies, they may be a candidate for gender-affirming care. Finally, he believes it is important that public schools employ educators, principals, and administrators, from the top down, who support transgender and non-binary affirming care. Again, that should not be their role. They should only be charged with educating them in academic subjects and helping them prepare for college or a trade school.

To be fair, FactCheck.org has an article by Kate Yandell posted on May 23, 2023. entitled, "Young Children Do Not Receive Medical Gender Transition Treatment." The author refutes the allegations made by Ms. Rachmuth and her organization, Education First Alliance North Carolina, that Duke, UHC, and ECU are providing gender-affirming care to minors. Ms. Yandell said in her article, "Representatives from all three North Carolina institutions referenced in the social media posts told us via emailed statements that they do not offer surgeries or other transition treatments to toddlers."

Yet, on their website, Edfirstnc.org, Sloan Rachmuth, in their article on June 6, 2023, "Duke Doctor Giving Puberty Blockers To Second Graders," stated, "Duke doctor Deanna Adkins admitted she gave puberty blockers to 8-year-old patients during a recent interview with the North Carolina Medical Society." Ms. Rachmuth, in her article on May 5, 2023, entitled "Panic Mode: Duke & UNC Deny ECU Wrongdoing In Treating Transgender Toddlers," wrote, "According to Croft, the UNC Pediatric and Adolescent Clinic for Gender Wellness administers puberty blockers to children as young as 11 years old."

Finally, in Ms. Rachmuth's article on May 10, 2023, entitled "ECU To Sue Education First Alliance For Reporting Its Gender Clinic," she wrote there is a "video of this year's faculty convocation where the chair of the Sexual and Gender Committee boasted about bringing pediatric "gender-affirming care" to ECU. Guess who was sitting 15 feet away, grinning and nodding, approving? ECU chancellor, Phillip Rogers." Also, at this same conference, ECU's director of pediatric medical research proclaimed that ECU Health CEO Michael Waldrum and Brody Med School Dean Jason Higginson were an intimate part of planning its "gender-affirming care clinic for all ages."

Speaking of Vanderbilt Hospital, the following is from an article from The Conservative Post from September 21, 2022, entitled, "Vanderbilt Hospital: Gender Reassignment a 'Money Maker,' Threatens Doctors Who Object." The article cites an investigation conducted by Matt Walsh, an American conservative commentator, author, and podcaster. The article states that Mr. Walsh "shows how gender reassignment has been promoted as a 'big money maker' and also reveals alleged threats posed by hospital leaders against medical professionals who opposed performing the surgeries due to religious beliefs." The article continued by noting, "Dr. Shayne Taylor helped launch Vanderbilt's gender clinic in 2018 and admitted in a lecture delivered that same year that sex-change treatments were very profitable. She noted that insurance carriers are required under Obamacare to cover "medical expenses for trans folks." She bragged that every gender-confused woman who wishes to undergo "top surgery," otherwise known as a double mastectomy" and also what is known as "bottom surgeries." The article states, "the hospital has promoted giving those as young as 13 years old irreversible hormone therapy."

However, in 2023, it appears that state legislators and governors may be in agreement on banning gender-affirming surgeries and care (which would include prescribing puberty blockers and hormones) to minors under the age of 18. Tennessee appears to be the first state to enact such a law. Other states like Nebraska, Mississippi, Oklahoma, South Dakota, Utah, Alabama, and Arkansas are considering similar legislation. It is hard to believe that state legislators would have to pass bills to prevent hospitals and doctors from conducting gender-changing surgeries and giving hormones to minors.

However, on April 20, 2023, the American Civil Liberties Union and LGBTQ group Lambda Legal filed a lawsuit seeking to strike down this new Tennessee law that bans doctors from providing gender-affirming medical treatment such as puberty blockers, hormone therapy, and surgery to transgender minors. Tennessee state representative Gloria Johnson made this comment regarding the bill and minors, "If a doctor and a family feels that taking hormone blockers is going to be healthy and productive and life-saving for these children, that's a decision that should be made," The issue missing from Ms. Johnson comment is that minors that are considering gender-affirming care should be receiving therapy for gender dysphoria until they are 18. It is possible that therapy and living their life, along with the passage of time, age, and wisdom, might persuade them to accept the gender they were assigned at birth. According to a poll conducted by Trafalgar in October of 2022, 78.7% of Americans believe that transgender surgery should be postponed until the individual is at least 18 years of age.

From the discussion above, one might assume that the prescribing of hormone or puberty blockers might be an alternative to gender-changing surgeries while the child or adolescent is in therapy or until they become an adult. However, there is evidence, even acknowledged by the Food and Drug Administration about the harmful effects of such medications. In an article from the Independent Women's Forum written by Zoe Forest on June 23, 2023, entitled, "HHS Refuses To Follow The Science On Puberty Blockers," she wrote that in 2022, Reuters reported, "Puberty blockers and sex hormones do not have US Food and Drug Administration (FDA) approval for children's gender care. No clinical trials have established their safety for such off-label use. The drugs' long-term effects on fertility and sexual function remain unclear. In 2016, the FDA ordered makers of puberty blockers to add a warning about psychiatric problems to the drugs' label after the agency received reports of suicidal thoughts in children who were taking them." She also stated that the FDA in 2022 has admitted that these medications may cause swelling in the brain and permanent vision loss. Finally, she reported that the NY Times in November 2022 that those minors who take these medications are at risk of developing osteoporosis. So, the question that should be asked is, are parents made aware of the risks of having these medications prescribed to their minors?

Countries like Finland, Sweden, Norway, the UK, New Zealand, Australia, and France have banned gender-affirming care and surgeries or severely limited these practices. Dr. Miriam Grossman stated that the claims that social and medical treatments toward gender-affirming care, if not adhered to, would lead children to commit suicide. She said that several countries have banned this care to minors, and there has been "no wave of suicides or other mental health catastrophes."

Dr. Grossman further asserted that prominent experts in the field of transgenderism and treating these patients and publishing papers on the subject for many years, such as Dr. Stephen Levine, Dr. Kenneth Zucker, Dr. Paul McHugh, Dr. James Cantor, and others. Clinicians and other disciplines who have wisdom and experience are ignored because they disagree with the current narrative. They are against these medical interventions for the same reasons as the seven countries mentioned above. She advocates psychotherapy for those individuals, minors, and adults for anyone struggling with accepting their gender at birth. The sessions would explore the client's feelings, irrational thinking, perhaps their social anxiety, influence, and addiction to social media platforms. The therapist would conduct a very thorough psycho-social evaluation, including interviewing the parents, teachers, and school counselors. The purpose of counseling is not to rubber-stamp the minors' request for gender-affirming care (puberty blockers, hormone injections, surgery, etc.).

So, once gender-altering surgery has been performed, how many regret their decision? In an article from Human Life International entitled, "How Many Trans People Regret Transitioning?" author Susan Ciancio reported a 2015 US Transgender Survey, "the most recent available because of the pandemic—claims that 11% of female respondents reverted back to their original sex. Transgender men had a reversion rate of 4%. Those who chose to revert cited a variety of reasons. Five percent of those who detransitioned realized that a gender transition was not what they wanted. Other people cited family pressure and difficulty getting a job as reasons to detransition."

But here is a more recent study published in 2024 by Groningen University from the Netherlands. The article entitled "Gender doubts are a normal part of growing up," found only "one in 10 young teens who express a wish to change gender 'grows out it' and may benefit more from psychological help than gender alignment treatment." There were 2700 youngsters who were part of the study, and they were inquired "about their wish at different ages. At age 11, some 10% said they wanted to change gender. That had dropped to just 4% by the time they had reached 25." Researchers also found that "depression and low self-esteem played a big role in the initial wish." Psychologist and head researcher Sarah Burke said, "During puberty, teens are looking for an identity. They have all sorts of doubts and questions. So, it's understandable. Expressing a wish to change gender at a young age does not mean the person is transgender and can be part of growing up." Medical ethics expert Jilles Smids said, "The study shows medical intervention is not necessary in the majority of the cases. It's normal to have doubts about your gender." Two additional points can be gleaned from this study: Our society needs more understanding when it comes to minors who have doubts about their gender, that this is a normal phase in their development, and that children who think they are in the wrong body are referred to gender-changing clinics too quickly. The professionals making these referrals don't have enough knowledge on child development to help these children.

So, back to Ms. Ciancio. She also referenced the "authors of a 2021 article in Plastic and Reconstructive Surgery conducted a systematic review of several databases to determine the rate of regret for those who had undergone surgery. According to the article, '7928 transgender patients who underwent any type of [gender-affirmation surgeries] were included. The pooled prevalence of regret after

GAS was 1% (95% CI <1%–2%). FYI: When I wrote this book, the 1% regret rate combined minors and adults. I believe that the statistic may be accurate in that 1% of adults who have had gender-affirming surgeries, maybe 1% regretted having the irresistible surgeries. However, I contend that the incidence of minors regretting these surgeries will increase as they become adults. Ms. Ciancio continued by saying, " 'However, the article goes on to state that there was "high subjectivity in the assessment of regret and lack of standardized questionnaires, which highlight the importance of developing validated questionnaires in this population.'" Ms. Ciancio states that the low number of trans people who regret having their surgery believe there is more than what is being reported, and they fear speaking up. Many who are speaking up are noting that they are unhappy with their new gender.

Finally, Ms. Ciancio included actual quotes from those who expressed their regrets. "A woman named Ruby who had undergone testosterone therapy and lived as a male. However, she changed her mind about transitioning to a male before she was scheduled to have surgery to remove her breasts. Ruby states: "'I didn't think any change was going to be enough in the end, and I thought it was better to work on changing how I felt about myself than changing my body. I've seen similarities in the way I experience gender dysphoria, in the way I experience other body image issues."

Here is another example of an individual regretting his decision to transition from a male to a female. The following came from an article from an online publication called "JOE." The article is entitled, Influencer Who Transitioned Into A Korean Woman Is Now Transitioning Back Into A British Man," by Steve Hopkins, December 11, 2022. In the article, Oli London was interviewed, and he "admitted it was a mistake to identify as "transracial." Oli London was quoted as, "I realise that was a big mistake, and I just want to be a boy," the 32-year-old said, "but is it any wonder people like me and young people want to change their gender when we have normalisation of this in our schools in this country." He continued: "Children are taught from a young age, from the age of five in some cases, that it's okay to change their gender, it's okay to wear a skirt, it's okay for a boy to use the gender-neutral toilet when it puts girls at risk." He has had 30 surgeries and has spent more than $271,000 over an eight-year period.

8-2 An Adolescent with Non-Dysphoria Symptoms

A female colleague shared the following case with me. The colleague stated that her 14-year-old female client came from divorced parents. This colleague obtained this referral from the parents and the adolescent's school counselor. The teen reported being bullied and ridiculed at school by female peers for having small breasts. She admitted to viewing social media sites that only contributed to her low self-esteem because the sites she viewed did not embrace the virtues of being a female and the traits of femineity. The adolescent admitted to the counselor that all of these incidents led her to question what it meant to be a female. The client and her parents said the teenager never espoused any symptoms of gender dysphoria. So, the therapist stated she began counseling with this teen not as someone who was struggling with gender dysphoria but as someone who was experiencing the typical issues of being a female adolescent and dealing with sometimes cruel peers and negative feedback from social media sites.

So, whether it is the client I just described or clients like Ruby or Oli London, I envision our role is to provide counseling. Rather than providing "gender-affirming therapy," an ethical therapist would have a non-biased discussion with the client and attempt to help them arrive at a decision, not just in the short term but one that they will not regret for years to come. One factor that no one seems to be adding to the discussion is that children and adolescents are impulsive. They do not fully comprehend or seek out all experts before making a life-altering decision. To further make the point, why don't we, as a society, allow minors to do virtually anything they want legally? Here is a partial list of things minors can't do: they can't vote, sign contracts, buy property, cannot access inheritances, cannot buy cigarettes or alcohol, and they cannot get a tattoo or body piercing unless a parent or guardian consents.

In a perfect world, neither parents nor medical professionals would not even consider gender-altering surgery for any minors. There would be a permanent halt on these types of surgeries until the age of at least 18. Regarding counseling, again, children considering transgender affirming care of any kind should be required to be in therapy until they become adults before they can legally make those decisions. Furthermore, even adults who want transgender-affirming care should be directed to psychotherapy for perhaps a year, especially if they wish for transgender surgery because those changes are irreversible once performed.

It seems like the mental health profession has become quite liberal and, in some cases, quite radical. It is forcing clinicians to accept and implement everything contained in this chapter without considering if these mandates are for the betterment of society. After having presented all these topics in this chapter, when it comes to counseling clients, I try to work with the majority of folks requesting services. I believe we, as clinicians, can provide good therapy without following all the trappings of pitting races and cultures against one another, as evidenced in the book I referenced on cultural diversity and wokeism.

However, after having stated all the above in this chapter, you have to be honest and inform a client if you lack experience in dealing with their presenting issue. In 1973, in the movie Magnum Force," Clint Eastwood's character Harry Callahan, famous quote: "A man has to know his limitations." In this instance, the quote meant that clinicians should be aware of their own strengths and those that aren't. They should not overestimate their abilities or act beyond their competencies. In those cases, it would be ethical to help them find a colleague who can help those clients accomplish their goals. And that is true in all situations. For instance, I have no training or certification in play therapy or Eye movement desensitization and reprocessing (EMDR). Therefore, if a client required those services, I would need to refer them to someone who could meet their needs.

CHAPTER 9:

So, You Really Want To Establish Your Very Own Private Practice

IN CHAPTER 2, I offered a lot of advice to new clinicians. In this chapter, I want to specifically address and offer advice to those wishing to establish their private practice. But, again, I want to remind you of the same recommendation I suggested in Chapter 2: consider working in settings where you can obtain both experience and supervision for several years before embarking on a private practice.

To remind you of my story, I had always wanted a private practice. My goal was to establish a full-time practice as soon as possible after I had acquired many years of experience and believed I no longer needed supervision. However, after working at a for-profit counseling business, where I was required to see 35 clients out of a 40-hour week, I decided against establishing a full-time practice in favor of keeping my 40-hour day job and my part-time private practice. Before making this decision, I consulted with several clinicians who had successful full-time private practices. I asked them for advice on how they established their practices into a full-time endeavor. Their reply scared me and caused me many sleepless nights as they advised me just to quit my day job and ramp up my practice from part-time to full-time. I never regretted my decision to keep my full-time day job and private practice part-time of seeing my own clients in the evenings, as I had the best of both worlds. Now that I am retired, I have continued my private practice part-time.

There are advantages to having a private practice. First, it is your own business, where you are your own boss and have complete autonomy. Second, you can decide on the kind and how many clients to see in a day and for the week. However, I need to mention some downsides to establishing and maintaining a private practice. It does require more responsibility and liability and can be isolating and overwhelming. Yes, you work independently, but your practice will also take hard work, time, and money.

As you have decided to establish your practice, you will need to decide whether to practice with other clinicians with whom you share a common waiting room or join an established group where there are individuals or partners. In this scenario, the individual clinicians get a percentage or set amount from each client they see. In addition, you need to decide whether to join insurance panels and/or contract with managed care companies that provide Employee Assistance Programs (EAPs) to their member clients vs. only accepting private pay from your clients. Of course, if you choose to be on insurance panels and/or are contracted with managed care (EAPs), you will have to accept what the contract you have entered into will pay you. In addition to the lower pay, you may have the required paperwork to complete. Finally, some clinicians will offer a sliding fee scale to their clients, where their finances are considered as to what they can pay and what the clinician will charge per session.

There are many advantages to private pay. There are fewer restrictions and little to no paperwork to complete. If you only accept private compensation or have clients who don't have insurance, you will need to determine how much you will charge per session. These clinicians choose not to be on insurance panels or contracted with managed care companies. Also, they are more selective about the clients they want to see and perhaps have established a niche or specialty that sets them apart from other practitioners. Again, I typically see new intakes for as long as 90 minutes, whether or not they have insurance or if they came to me through their EAP. I know I will not be paid for seeing these clients for longer than an hour. But I believe it would be a disservice to say to a client or couple, after I have seen them for an hour and have only gathered info about their presenting issue and their information, to complete my intake form without also providing some therapy and giving them at least one homework assignment. I charge more for clients who pay for counseling out of pocket for their first session because I typically see a first-time client between 75 and 90 minutes.

What Is Required

So, let's drill down what is required of the private practice clinicians as they are establishing their own practice. First, of course, it is a given that they must be licensed in the state where they will be practicing. Second, you must also have malpractice insurance; the minimal coverage is $1 million for "Individual–Each Incident" and $3 million for "Aggregate." Third, I recommend obtaining a Tax ID called an Employer Identification Number (EIN). One can use their Social Security Number, but I advise separating their private practice income and expenses from their personal ones. Next, they need to obtain a National Provider Identifier number, which is required if they are in private practice, accept insurance, or are on managed care. Fourth, those taking insurance will want to register their practice with CAQH ProView. Many insurance companies use CAQH as the source to obtain information about you that you submit on CAQH's website. The information you would provide would include your licensure information and when it expires, your National Identifier Number (NPI), your Tax ID, your current malpractice information, the address where you practice, and the hours you are available to see clients. Finally, some colleagues will advise you to obtain a business and register it as an LLC, which stands for Limited Liability Company or a PLLC (Professional Limited Liability Company. They also provide potential tax savings unavailable to sole proprietorships or partnerships.

Establishing Your Own Office

Suppose you want your private practice to be in an office; do you know where you want your office to be located? You have heard the expression, "location, location, location." I believe this applies to deciding where you want to practice. In my case, I chose a location on the service road of a major freeway, which is convenient for clients living in North Dallas and many surrounding suburbs around Dallas, to the north, west, and east. Another option to having your own office and paying monthly rent to a landlord is to pay a clinician by the hour or sublease the time they are not using their office. This could help you to transition and ease into a full-time practice. As your practice grows, you continue to pay for the time you need an office from a colleague until you justify the need for your own office, either part-time or full-time.

Expenses of a Private Practice

So, we covered the expense of an office. Now, let's talk about the other costs of your private practice office. In that case, here are some things you will need to order. If you use any inventories, such as the Beck Depression inventory, you will need to include the expenses. You will also need office supplies (including legal pads, pens, pencils, a clipboard, a stapler, Scotch tape, boxes of tissues, and at least one clock), a lockable file cabinet, lamps, a shredder, etc.

Other expenses include setting aside money to fund your health insurance and retirement if you are going to take your practice full-time. Some clinicians decide it is worth the cost of having the internet in their office. I decided against it because I wanted to keep my costs low, and my practice is part-time. Additional expenses include continuing educational units (CEUs) and any fees associated with professional organizations you choose to join. Some choose to have a separate cell phone from their personal one. Other expenses include any advertisement of your practice, taxes, licensing costs, and malpractice. If the office is not furnished, you will need a desk and furniture for your clients. Here are some other items related to your financial goals to consider: how much money you will need to bring in to meet expenses, make a living, and allow you to keep practicing. Consider establishing the goals of your practice for the first few months, the first year, and the first few years after that.

Arranging Your Office

The following is how I have my office arranged: I operate my office with lamps instead of using overhead lighting. I position the clock(s) on the wall above clients so that I can keep track of the session time. In my office, you will find my desk and a chair that swivels. I stay in that chair to conduct my sessions. For my clients, I have a loveseat and a wingback chair. I have tables next to the chair, the loveseat, and lamps on each table. I have boxes of tissues next to the sofa and the chair. I also have bookcases for reference books and other books I can acquaint clients with, such as the one with 1001 Romantic Ideas. Then, on the walls, you will display your license(s) and any certifications you have earned. Finally, you will need to display on your wall how clients can initiate a complaint to the licensing board through the license(s) you possess.

Required & Suggested Forms For Your Practice

When you meet with a client for the first time, you must have them sign a Consent to Treatment form before you conduct and complete the intake. You cannot initiate therapy without their signature. I also have them complete a Demographic Client Form titled "Welcome To My Office." On that form, I have enclosed the date the client first contacted me, their name, and date of birth. If the client is a minor, I ask them who their parent or guardian is and their address and cell number. If they are using insurance, what is their member ID number, insurance company name, and telephone number? If there is a deductible, how much of it has been satisfied, and after that, what is the copay? If they are using their EAP, the name of their EAP, their 800 number, the authorization number, the number of sessions being authorized, and the range of dates are approved. I would include the spouse or significant other (if they will be joining the client) and their date of birth on this form. Finally, on this form, I have the client include the referral source, why counseling is being requested, and all participants' signatures.

Let's return to the Consent to Treatment form, which is also known as The Statement of Understanding that you have required clients to sign before therapy commences. At the top of this form, I would suggest your letterhead. Next would be information about your practice and the services you provide. My statement on this form is as follows: "I am a licensed psychotherapist who believes that human beings are strong and resilient. They can survive many traumatic circumstances and still be able to lead satisfactory lives, heal, and learn healthy coping skills. Eventually, they will be able to "therapy" themselves. I am committed to providing the most proficient and sophisticated treatment available."

Next, in your Consent to Treatment form, you would address confidentiality and its limits. Here is my statement, "I am also committed to protecting your privacy. This means no one will know you are a client here unless you choose to tell them or you permit me to break your confidentiality. There are some exceptions to confidentiality, and they are (a) if you are a minor and you are being abused. (b) if you are engaging in, or planning to engage in, behavior that threatens the life of yourself or someone else. (c) if the court orders me. (d) if you are a minor and your parents insist on the information. However, I always enter into an agreement with parents at the first session that they respect your therapy privacy."

Continuing on the Informed Consent form, you would address if they have insurance or managed care (an EAP) by stating the following: "I may need to provide information regarding your care to your insurance carrier or managed care provider/reviewer. If I file insurance for you, please be informed that verification of insurance benefits with your insurance benefits does not guarantee payment by your insurance company. Any remaining balance will be your responsibility."

My next section on the Consent to Treatment form addresses Appointments: "Therapy appointments are 45-50 minutes in length. Your therapy time is reserved for you. Please notify me if you have to cancel your appointment at least 24 hours in advance. If 24 hours' notice is not given, your regular fee will be charged."

The next area on the form pertains to Payment of Fees: "The agreed payment is due at the end of each therapy session unless otherwise arranged in advance. Occasionally, an emergency requires telephone counseling. While you are encouraged to telephone in an emergency, please be informed that you will be charged for telephone time in excess of that required to set appointments."

Finally, in the last two sections, you would include your availability and their signature(s): "You can contact me through my cell phone, 214-728-0009, which has both voice mail and texting capability. When I am out of town, coverage will be arranged with one of my capable associates. By signing below, you verify you have read, understood, and agree to abide by the above policies." While other clinicians may have a Consent to Treatment form or a Statement of Understanding form that is multiple pages, mine is still 1 page.

Habits To Consider

I want to encourage new clinicians to establish and implement habits in their private practice. I usually see my clients in the mid-afternoon and early evening. My first habit is to call or text all my clients in the morning to remind them or confirm their appointment, and I request that they confirm by calling or texting me that they intend to keep their session. The next one, which I have already covered, is how much time you will devote to seeing new clients for the intake and the length of time you see return clients. Again, I often devote up to 90 minutes to conduct the intake. Then, I set aside time to complete the intake write-up before seeing my next client. I hold return clients to that 45–50-minute hour, giving myself time to complete the progress note before my next appointment. So, if it would help, you could schedule clients 30 minutes apart from each other to ensure you had time to complete the intake or progress note, return any calls between sessions, etc. This may also help you to clear your mind from one client to another and also gives you time to review your next client's progress notes, goals, and any homework assignments from the previous session.

Another habit I encourage new clinicians to adopt if they submit for their own reimbursement with insurance or managed care companies is to set aside time toward that endeavor at the end of each month. Then, I submit a note in the client's chart that I submitted for services rendered to the insurance or managed care company and another note in the chart when I receive a check or the check is directly deposited into my bank account.

Other Recommendations To Ponder

Speaking of seeing clients again, as you decide how many clients you will see in a day, you will need to consider whether you want to start in the morning and end in the afternoon or start in the afternoon and finish in the early evening. For example, in my part-time practice, I have chosen to see no more than three clients daily, and I want to keep my appointments close together without having large gaps in my schedule.

In addition to other recommendations regarding your private practice, you will need to keep track of your income and expenses.

I use Excel spreadsheets for both. Please consider using either a tax accountant to handle your private practice or a product like Turbo Tax to address your personal and private practice business. I have separate checking accounts and credit cards for both my private practice and individual needs. I am proud to say that I have never used any personal funds to augment my private practice; it has always been self-sustaining.

I stated earlier that your practice will require hard work, time, and money. The hard work would include all efforts to ensure your practice is thriving and viable, such as marketing your practice. The time also required consists of the time you will need to spend outside of counseling your clients. It would include completing intakes, progress notes (if you didn't finish them after each session), any paperwork required of you if you are contracted with any managed care groups, and letting others know about your practice. In addition, if you take care of your own filing for reimbursement with insurance or managed care companies if you are contracted with them, that will also require extra time.

If you are on insurance or managed care provider panels, you can decide to allow a company or individual to do that service instead of you doing your own billing. To help you with this decision, you would consider what percent you are willing to part with if you were to allow someone or a company to bill for your service. It is worth it for some clinicians to have someone else bill and ensure that the insurance or managed care company reimburses the clinician. Some clinicians hire the same group to obtain the benefits information for the clients they are scheduled to see.

The benefits information would include if the client has only insurance or if they also have an EAP (managed care). If the client has insurance, does the client have a deductible, and if so, how much of the deductible has been met? Then, what is the copay after the client meets their deductible? Suppose the client has an EAP, then the therapist has to ascertain this information from the managed care company. In that case, the clinician will need to know the authorization number, how many sessions are authorized, the date the authorization begins, and the date the authorization expires.

Then, there is the marketing of your practice. You may consider advertising in the Yellow Pages, but advertising there did not give me much bang for the buck. A colleague informed me about her success in advertising through Psychology Today, and it has been very helpful in obtaining new clients. You can use Facebook, Twitter, and other online platforms to promote your practice. Another suggestion is to construct your own web page. You could give presentations on mental health topics, such as stress management, to your church or synagogue while simultaneously informing them about your practice. You could consider meeting with a psychiatrist at their office or taking them out to lunch and exchanging information about each other's practices, which could lead to a referral base. You can utilize the same strategy in contacting doctors, attorneys, and anyone you can think of to ensure they are informed that you have established a private practice. The most essential marketing strategy is a no-brainer. Do good work, and help your clients accomplish their therapeutic goals. Former clients who speak your praises will refer friends and family members to your practice. They may also share how good you are to their physician, attorney, and other professionals.

Another suggestion is to talk with other clinicians who have successfully established and maintained their practice. Then, network with them. You can form a peer supervision group where you discuss challenging cases and share recommendations for a successful practice. Networking can help replace the support you received when you were employed and can help you with your feeling alone, which is one of the downsides of having a private practice. You will find that other therapists would be happy to join a peer support group. Again, attending CEUs is another way to network with colleagues, and the trainings will assist you in learning new skills or honing ones you already possess. All of these endeavors will create a healthy mental attitude that will sustain you as you establish your practice and maintain it for years to come.

Regarding expenses, I want to address a couple of last issues to keep in mind. Again, in private practice, you are required to maintain malpractice insurance. Most insurance companies that offer malpractice insurance base their premiums on how many clients you will see weekly. So, of course, the more clients you see a week, the higher the premium. In addition, in my situation, it may not be unique. Still, in the building where I have an office, not only do I pay rent, but the landlord also requires liability insurance, which, of course, is another expense.

So, to summarize, a clinician in private practice does not have to commit themselves to solely having a full-time practice; they can keep their practice part-time while holding down a full-time employer-paid salary with benefits. In addition, some therapists augment their counseling practice and income with other endeavors. For example, they may teach some psychology or counseling courses at a local college, conduct presentations or Critical Incident Stress Debriefings to company employees, or be a business consultant.

CHAPTER 10:

Additional Tips, Strategies & Final Thoughts

SO FAR, I have attempted to provide advice, offer metaphors and analogies, and visualizations on how clinicians can see their role in providing therapy to their clients. Here is one I often use. Imagine, as the therapist, you are playing an imaginary chess game with your client. You are asking the client questions, and as they answer them, you are putting together hypotheses. Then, in that imaginary chess game, you anticipate their moves as you plan your next ones. Just like in chess, you have alternate paths or movements based on the direction the client chooses. I am always ahead of the client on the following questions I want to ask. It is okay if one of your conclusions is corrected by your client. You would ask the client to rephrase and then say, "So, if I understand you correctly, you are saying..." Try to remain in control of your sessions, always ready to ask the next question or summarize either what the client has said or the direction the session has taken. At the end of the session, I almost always give a homework assignment and ask if this is a good place to stop before scheduling the next appointment.

In Chapter 6, I encouraged clinicians not to be intimidated by a client's presenting issue. There have been specific kinds of cases that I would not want my private practice to comprise, such as adults who abuse children or perpetrators of rape or borderline personality disorders. Many years ago, there was a case I could not avoid of having to counsel a client who certainly made me feel uncomfortable, at least initially.

10-1 Counseling A Client Convicted Of Rape

While I was a counselor at Personal Performance Consultants, there were four clinicians, including me, who were assigned cases. So, I was given the following case, and I was told this male client had been paroled from prison for rape. Upon seeing him initially, I asked my usual question, "How can I be of assistance to you?" And his reply was, "I was sent to prison for raping a woman." I inquired about the details of what he had done. He said he had driven alongside a woman and pointed to her car tire as though the tire was going flat. When she pulled over, that was when he raped her. Internally, I was repulsed by what he had just revealed. He wanted to examine why he had the compulsion to force a woman to have sexual intercourse against her will. He wanted counseling to confront and extinguish the compulsion. As I continued asking him more questions unrelated to what he had done that sent him to prison, I began seeing him in a different light. Yes, what he had done was repulsive, but eventually, I could see Yes, what he had done was repulsive, but eventually, I could see his redeeming qualities. I applauded his goal of ensuring he never would act on his compulsion again.

We discussed how the horrific act occurred. He admitted that he had been frequenting strip clubs and abusing alcohol. He was not able to initially understand that going to strip clubs had led him to devalue women. I referred him to AA, and while attending meetings, he decided to remain abstinent from alcohol. He also decided he would never frequent strip clubs ever again. Finally, I referred him to a colleague who specialized in working with perpetrators and said he would put this him in one of his groups. Again, this client and this case were a challenge to me. I was able to successfully provide counseling to a client who initially made me feel uncomfortable. Still, I was able to adequately assess the presenting issues, make progress with the client after a few sessions, and make appropriate referrals.

Never Assume A Client's Presenting Issue Is Always Psychological

As long as I continue to counsel, I will never forget the following example I would like to share with you.

10-2: Always Conduct A Thorough Assessment To Rule Out Any Medical Causes

A male client who was in his 40s requested counseling. He stated that his job was in construction, and often, he would be asked by one of his colleagues to bring back to them a particular tool. He said about a month ago, they were working in a high-rise building, and when he got to the toolbox, he forgot what he was asked to retrieve and the floor they were working on. He stated this was happening more frequently. He was requesting counseling to help him to improve his memory. Rather than agreeing to help him achieve his goal, it seemed imperative that I conduct a thorough assessment. I then inquired when he had last seen his medical doctor for a complete physical, which he said had been many years ago. I told him I did not feel comfortable providing therapy before we ruled out if there was a medical explanation for his symptoms.

I was able to persuade him to see his doctor ASAP. The next phone call I received was from his wife. She said her husband's doctor ordered an immediate MRI, which revealed he had a brain tumor. Then, an emergency surgery was performed. The wife thanked me for saving her husband's life. The surgeon had informed her that surgery would not have been an option if the operation had been delayed much longer.

This reinforced how important it is to ask clients about their current and past medical issues, when the last time their physician conducted a thorough physical, and if any prescribed medications are controlling their symptoms. Again, it is imperative as clinicians that we always perform a comprehensive assessment. Afterward, refer them to a physician if there is a question that the presenting problem needs to be ruled out medically first.

Counseling Clients With Work-related Issues

Some time ago, I began counseling a client who was put on a Performance Improvement Plan at work, and it reminded me of the skills I learned while employed with the Federal EAP. In counseling employed clients, the subject almost always comes up in their work. I encourage clients to meet with their supervisors at least once a month or as often as once a week. During this meeting, they should ask their supervisor about their performance and satisfaction. The client will also ask the employer if there are things that the client needs to improve or anything about their performance. Knowing what improvements must occur during these planned meetings is better than waiting for the yearly evaluation. If they wait until the annual performance evaluation, the client/employee has no time to make any required improvements. If the supervisor offers items that need improvement, then the client/employee can ask the supervisor for progress reports at each subsequent meeting.

10-3: An Example Of A Client With Work-related Issues

A male client requested counseling after recently being passed over for a supervisor position to which he had applied. He admitted he was angry about not being promoted to supervisor, which led him to be verbally reprimanded for remarks to both management and occasional customers. Through counseling, I was able to help with his anger in appropriate ways. However, the client and I also dealt with some workplace issues. For instance, he stated that although it was published in the company's policies and procedures manual that he was to have performance evaluations after many months of employment, he still needed one. This client was taught how to ask his supervisor diplomatically for performance evaluations (both in areas where he was meeting expectations but where he needed to improve). He was also encouraged to ask for regular meetings with his manager to continue to discuss his performance.

In sessions, this client also said that in his company, there is no mechanism to discuss possible scenarios and solutions that can be included in the company's policies and procedures nationwide. The client was so excited by this discussion that he was motivated to take suggestions to management and ask the company to consider trainings, blogging, and other ways to disseminate this information to employees and supervisors.

I believe that employees can express whatever they need to with a supervisor, provided they show respect and pick and choose their words carefully. I want to offer the following example of an incident that occurred between a former supervisor and me.

10-4: My Own Example Of Dealing With My Supervisor

An agreement was reached between a federal agency's Point of Contact (POC) and me before I worked under my supervision. A complaint was levied against me, and both my supervisor and a federal POC called me to discuss it. I had no prior knowledge about the complaint before the call. During the call, I felt ambushed and believed my supervisor was not supporting me. After the call, I admit I was angry.

I wanted to call my supervisor immediately and express my anger, but I knew my anger would drown out any salient points I wanted to make. So, I decided to wait a week until the next supervision time with this manager. By this time, I was much more in control of my emotions. I asked if we could discuss the incident the week before with her, me, and the point of contact. I provided her with the details she didn't have and hadn't been allowed to offer them in the initial call. She said she could support me now that she had my side of the story. I was then able to make the following statement to her: "I know I am not perfect, and I am sure sometime in the future, someone will again complain about me. When that happens, would you please tell the complainant that you will call me first and discuss the complaint? Then, after you and I have addressed the complaint, we can call the point of contact and engage in a three-way conversation." She agreed with my proposal and said she could and would do so in the future.

Again, I controlled my emotions, picked my words carefully, and respected her as my supervisor. I see supervisors as humans, too, and I hope what transpired between us helped her be a better manager. A supervisor's role is to help employees be the best they can be and ensure they are happy employees by motivating them, encouraging retention, and encouraging them to move up in the organization if they desire.

I have also worked with clients applying for a job or promotion and expressed anxiety about the upcoming interview. They would admit their fear was due to whether the person interviewing them had the power to hire them. We would discuss that all the interview questions were about them, their strengths, experiences, etc. I encourage them to use the internet and query the common questions asked during a job interview, preparing them for virtually every question they could ask. They would then be ready for every question asked; it would be like knocking each one out of the ballpark with their answers. Then, I have them imagine that instead of the interview occurring in an office setting, it is happening in their living room or at a Starbucks, which is a much more comfortable environment. Their ability to change their negative self-talk about how they viewed the interview process was their choice, and once they did, it could significantly reduce their anxiety.

By the way, the opposite of strengths is not weaknesses. They just present challenges that can be made into strengths. This is how one can answer that in a job interview or in life in general. For example, when I became employed with the Federal EAP, about 65% of my job was to conduct presentations on mental health topics. Initially, my presentations were horrible. However, over time, I made my presentation skills a strength. Words have power, they have meaning, and every word has antonyms. For instance, growing up, my parents repeatedly called me "stubborn" until I learned I wasn't stubborn; I am "persistent." As I have shared many examples in this book, persistence has served me well in my career and in life. Sometimes, in the working world, supervisors will inform employees during a performance evaluation that they will offer "constructive criticism." Employees might say to themselves that they don't care how constructive the review is; the word they will focus on is "criticism." So, perhaps a better word to use instead of "criticism" is "feedback." So, let me bring it all together. Whether in work or between couples or parenting children, we all respond to positive words that motivate, increase our self-esteem, and lead us to strive to be our best.

Grief

While employed at the Federal EAP, I continued to hone my skills in providing grief counseling and conducting grief groups. Throughout our lives, we will all experience grief and loss. It is unavoidable. It could be the death of our parents, a beloved pet, or, worse, the death of a child or a spouse. Unfortunately, there are a lot of well-meaning friends and family members who will put a time limit on their grief. Most clients will get through their grief but at their own pace. In our grief, we all know that the first year is often the toughest due to holidays, birthdays, and other occasions we might have once celebrated. And now, we dread those occasions and remembrances.

So, one suggestion to offer to our clients regarding these upcoming occasions is to be proactive. Consider planning ahead to be busy, be with family and friends rather than staying alone, and consider changing how a holiday is encountered. Another suggestion is to choose to focus on positive memories. I actually encourage clients to write down as many memories as they can recall about their beloved and keep the list close by to refer to the list as often as needed. So, they can bring out the list whenever they dwell on the negative. Sometimes looking at happier memories may bring a smile rather than a tear. As time progresses, we tend to focus on how our loved ones lived rather than on how they died, that each person's life had meaning and significance. And, as time goes by, smiles may overtake the tears. Other recommendations include encouraging the client to return to their usual routine as quickly as possible: partaking in interests/hobbies, exercising (which also releases endorphins and other helpful brain chemicals), and not passing up opportunities to be with family and friends. Laughter, which also releases the same beneficial brain chemicals, is also helpful, or at least smiling can be just as therapeutic. After a funeral, grievers will recall stories, memories and laugh as they remember things about their loved one that will not be forgotten.

Another recommendation is to turn their grief into a cause. We have all heard about the Mothers Against Drunk Drivers (MADD) group. It was started by Candace (Candy) Lightner, the mother of a 13-year-old girl who was killed by a drunken hit-and-run driver. I had been counseling a grandmother who lost her grandson in a car accident. She decided to start a scholarship in his name at the university he was to attend. In conducting a grief group at an agency's work group, the colleagues decided to name the conference room to honor the deceased at the end of the meeting.

Reminding clients about resilience is also essential. Resilience is the ability to bounce back from adversity, setbacks, and grief. We tend to forget those things in our past that were a challenge to us. How we met those challenges can be successful templates to get through current and future ones. When I was conducting grief groups for the federal EAP, and when I provided counseling then, and now, I emphasized our ability to be resilient.

When my father was in hospice, a pamphlet was available to grievers. It is referred to as the "blue book" and is called "Gone From My Sight: The Dying Experience" by Barbara Karnes, and it is available to the public to order. The book is very beneficial as it lays out what one can expect as one deals with the eventual passing of their loved one as the person progresses from one stage to another before their death. As a therapist who helps paint mental pictures for my clients, I expanded the reference about the ship and the seashore in more detail. Therefore, I will say the following to clients as they are struggling with the death of a loved one. "Imagine you and many others (some you may know and others who are strangers to you) are standing at a pier, and tied to the dock is a very large ship. Onboard the ship are loved ones who are being grieved by others on the dock. We are waving goodbye to our respective loved ones. Then, the ship takes off toward the horizon as we continue to wave goodbye. Finally, the vessel is no longer seen as the boat crosses to the other side of the horizon. As the ship proceeds to that dock, those who have died previously are now waving hello to those onboard. We believe that one day, we will reunite again with those who have passed away before us." This passage has been a comfort for me. My clients often state that they also hope to see their loved ones in the future.

Losses

If I had one wish to grant my fellow colleagues, it would be that in their entire careers, they never have to deal with the death of a client, whether it is by accident, natural causes, or suicide. But, of course, that may be wishful thinking or a pipe dream. In nearly 40 years of counseling, I have encountered all three.

To my knowledge, I have only had one client who took their life while I was her therapist, and I still think about her often. There is a saying about suicide that it is a permanent solution to what is often a temporary problem. When I saw her for the initial intake appointment, she verbalized moderate depressive symptoms, and she denied any thoughts of wanting to harm herself. Nevertheless, she was resistant to being referred to a psychiatrist to be considered for an antidepressant. After seeing her for a few sessions, she said she believed the counseling was helping her, and her symptoms were improving. To this day, I am not sure what happened in between sessions. I am unsure if her overdose of medications in her medicine chest was accidental, a cry for help, or intentionally taking her life. Looking back on this client, I am unsure if she was honest with me when she said at each session that she had no suicidal ideations. Some comprehensive assessments can be utilized with clients you suspect and diagnose with Major Depression with Suicidal Ideations. Of course, with these individuals, I request that they admit themselves (or have a family member accompany them) to a psychiatric hospital where an antidepressant can be dispensed, and they can be on a suicide watch while the medication is getting them over the critical time period.

This next client case breaks my heart even 20 years later. This male client sought me out to provide counseling to him as part of the condition of his probation. He was on a 5-year probation for possession and selling cocaine. The conditions of his probation were for him to abstain from alcohol and all substances. He had only been married for two years, and his wife had given birth to their 10-month-old son. He was employed with an electric company installing and repairing electrical power lines. In one of his sessions, he disclosed what had happened at work. He said he was about to make repairs on a line when something told him to request that his supervisor ensure that the power to the line had been turned off. But in fact, the line was still alive. If he had not requested that his supervisor ensure the power to the line was turned off, he would have been electrocuted. Then, four months later, the client no-showed. When I called to check on him, his wife answered his phone and informed me that he had died while on the job restoring a power line after a winter storm. The client had disclosed the same thing earlier in the previous session. The power line he was working on should have been turned off; it wasn't, and he was electrocuted. Over the years, I have thought about this client. Yes, he had made a mistake that put him on probation, but he was succeeding in getting his life back on track. You could say after two years of marriage, he was still a newlywed with a 10-month-old son, who would grow up without any memories of his father.

Smoking Cessation

Self-Disclosure: Although I never smoked cigarettes, I did briefly smoke a pipe, partially because I enjoyed smelling pipe tobacco when someone else was smoking nearby. But it didn't take long for me to discover that I was not too fond of the taste when I smoked, and after I filled my pockets with pipe paraphernalia, I no longer had room for my wallet, keys, pocket change, etc.

We have all heard of smoking cessation programs and patches, but when I had my first client who wanted my assistance in helping him cease his cigarette habit, I never had any formal training in that area. However, I approached this challenge as I have done with others by using logic and CBT methods.

This client was smoking a pack of cigarettes a day. There are 20 cigarettes in a pack. So, I recommended that he reduce his habit to 19 cigarettes a day for a week. Each week, he would reduce the amount by 1. He could stretch that number throughout the day, but he could not increase the total number of cigarettes he took daily. As he was reducing the number of cigarettes he smoked per day, we also worked on the behavioral part of the equation. He motivated himself by using the money he was saving in an account to purchase something that was really desired. He also began exercising. He knew smoking would be a contradiction to living a healthier lifestyle and finding more beneficial things to do with his hands and to satisfy his oral fixation. Not only was this method successful for this client, but I also began using it with other clients with similar issues.

Again, feel free to challenge clients' presenting issues. Just like the medical model, we, as clinicians, shall do no harm to our clients. However, in those cases, we must admit when those clients need to be referred to a colleague with the training we lack. Some of my examples would include Eye Movement Desensitization and Reprocessing (EMDR) or hypnotherapy for any condition, such as PTSD or weight loss, to name a couple.

Weight Loss/Weight Management

Even though I do not have any training with hypnosis, I have had clients who asked for help with losing weight or weight management. So again, I would employ logic and CBT. As with any presenting issue, you want to complete a thorough assessment and ensure they have had a recent physical with their doctor. Of course, there are physical conditions and certain medications that contribute to their inability to lose or keep their weight off. Once you have ruled out that the client does not have any physical reasons or medicines that are at issue, then you could proceed by asking additional questions. Those inquiries would include: Was there a time when you found success in losing or keeping your weight off, such as exercising or participating in a particular sport? Was there a strategy that worked for you, such as keeping track of the foods consumed each day or calories consumed, etc.?

The purpose of these inquiries is to help the client find success in the methods they will use. In my case, as I have gotten older, I cannot keep my weight off as easily as when I was younger. As a result, I have a joke for virtually everything. You have heard of a metal detector; well, I need a sensor to find my metabolism! Since there isn't such a thing as a metabolism detector, my solution was to eat breakfast, lunch, and fruit in the late afternoon and evening but no dinner. Then, throughout the day and into the evening, I ensure I am adequately hydrated. This strategy has been successful for me. So again, the client and I are searching for what will work for them in accomplishing their goal.

What Happens When It Is Unavoidable In Taking A Client?

We learned in graduate school to avoid counseling clients when we first know them as individuals or, if we are doing business with them, to not take them on as clients. However, there were two situations where this was not possible, and I relied on my years of experience to get me through these two dilemmas.

The first situation occurred when I saw a female client for a few sessions before she revealed her best friend's name. When she told me the name of her best friend and the name was so unusual, I debated whether to say anything at all, but I decided I had to disclose it. My thought was what would happen if my client told her friend the name of her therapist. That convinced me I needed to reveal that I knew the friend because that friend was married to my wife's nephew. I informed the client that she could be assured that I would never tell her name to my nephew's wife, and if the client was okay with continuing counseling with me, I was okay seeing her as a client. She elected to continue seeing me in therapy, and we were able to accomplish her goals.

The second incident occurred similarly. I had been seeing a family for counseling for several sessions when they surprisingly showed up as friends at one of my wife's family functions. Talking with them was unavoidable, but the conversations were not substantiative at all. Then at their next appointment, we discussed how each of us knew the family from the party. The family felt comfortable continuing to see me to help them accomplish their goals, and I assured them that their confidentiality would continue to be protected. The clients stated that they did not want to start over with a new therapist and were pleased with their progress so far.

Other Healthy Strategies To Use with Clients

One visualization that can be used with clients is that of a "recipe card box." However, instead of putting recipe cards in the box, clients will have a separate box or container for each aspect of their life (job, marriage/relationship, parenting, etc.), and they will fill each one with successful strategies. How did those strategies become successful? Through trial and error. A specific approach is attempted, and there are three possible outcomes: one strategy was automatically successful; the second strategy, the process was unsuccessful after trying it a few or several times and should be abandoned. The third possibility was that the strategy that was tried needed to be tweaked. Once we find what works, our motto can be: my strategies work every time they are used; they cease to work only when I fail to use them.

As an example, I used to have a good memory once upon a time. But after forgetting to follow through on things I had promised, I had to admit my memory used to be different. So, I had to find a strategy that would work for me. For instance, if I promise a client I will complete something for them by their next appointment, I will likely not remember to complete the task if I don't write it down. Then, once I wrote down the tasks I needed to finish, it would also force me to complete them. Finally, I would take the completed assignment and put it in their chart, with the completed task sticking up to remind me to give it to them at their next session. So, again, each time we find successful strategies in each component of our lives, we put them in their respective "boxes."

Another strategy that clients can use is illustrating that their life is a book. All the pages on the left side of the book have already been written. That represents their past. And it doesn't benefit them much to focus on their history and regrets. So, instead, I encourage them to focus on what they have learned and what they will do differently in the future. Then I tell them the right side or the rest of the book's pages are all blank, representing the rest of their lives. And they are responsible for how those pages in their future are written. Some clients will say things like, "I am a product of how I was raised," as though there is nothing they can do; there is no free will. To contradict their way of accepting the negative, you say, "We had little control over our lives when we were children. You can refer to that part of your life as Part 1. Now that we are adults, we determine whether we keep using Part 1 of our life to prevent us from succeeding and seeing ourselves as continual victims. Anything we want to achieve from this point forward is up to us; there is free will."

Still, another strategy I use to describe our parents' (or anyone else who has had a positive influence in our lives) attributes and which ones to adopt when we become adults. So, I have clients visualize a "buffet." But instead of this being a food buffet, this is a buffet where you can pick and choose which one of our parents' attributes we want to adopt as we become adults. Just because there was a trait of our parents doesn't automatically mean we should decide to "put it on our plate," particularly if it was a negative one. As we got older, we realized that our parents were not perfect and not all their attributes were positive. So, we don't have to choose all their traits, particularly the negative ones. Ultimately, the qualities we adopt from our parents and those we acquire from life experiences through trial and error. As we mature, those qualities we choose "to put on our plates" can help us strive toward self-actualization, the best we can be.

Dr. Edwin Timmons, a professor at Louisiana State University in Baton Rouge, taught Adjustment Psychology, and I was very fortunate to attend his course. All these years later, some of his quotes still resonate with me: "We are all trying to get through this world the best way we know how." Second, "We often learn things through trial and error until we achieve our goals, which provides us reinforcement." Third, "We all strive to be somebody." Fourth, "Our need for achievement is knowing that we did our best even if no one else notices that achievement." And finally, "we put order in the world in order to make sense of the world." He used the concept that we present ourselves to others as "onions" and "onion skins." Our onion skins are who we are: a combination of coping skills, defense mechanisms, personality, temperament, fears, anxiety, goals, motivators, likes, and dislikes. As opportunities are presented, whether with clients or conducting presentations, I continue to immortalize him by reciting his quotes to my clients.

What I Learned In The History Of Psychology Course

A long-time professor, Dr. Robert Vidulich, taught the History of Psychology course at what was once Memphis State University (now referred to as the University of Memphis). It was one of the most exciting courses I took as an undergraduate. This professor arrived at each class, lecturing without any notes. He would talk about individuals who influenced the field of psychology in each class. The students could almost see him discussing them in a way they had never seen before. His stories were so interesting that sometimes, I laid my pen down, forgetting to take notes. I had been under the mistaken belief that the history of psychology only went back to the time of Freud. Instead, I learned that psychology and philosophy were intertwined with the likes of Plato, Socrates, and Aristotle. And the questions these early philosophers asked, we continue to inquire today.

The questions that were entertained were about the essence of man (and woman), the limitations of our knowledge, and our morals and ethics. Even back then, there was an emphasis on "know thyself," "to be introspective," and "to reason with yourself." In addition, there was a belief in the Philosophy of Aspiration, which was to maximize our potential and strive toward self-actualization. In the same way, I want my clients to achieve this in my therapy sessions. I tell them that I want to be a vehicle to help attain these goals.

What Makes Life Worth Living

Once upon a time, I worked with a woman who was part of the agency's support staff. Everything I am going to share was true about her. She was a widow; she had adult children and never spoke about her visiting them or they visiting her. She was the first to arrive at work and the last to leave, and she also lived across the street from work. When she couldn't sleep at night, she said she came to work because there was always work to be completed after all. She never talked about having interests, hobbies, or friends. What happens to this former colleague when work is a stressor or she decides to retire? Work was her universe. Work represented 100% of her life. Here's another example: there are some individuals who are married and work and do not have any other aspects of their lives. Their work and marriage represent 50% of their life.

The healthiest individuals are the ones who have the following components in their lives. However, they are not in any particular order: Marriage; and if they are not married, they have a relationship with their significant other, or they are striving to find a relationship with that individual (I always say kiddingly that it is okay to have a relationship with one's spouse, it is okay to have a relationship with a significant other but it is not okay to have a sexual relationship with someone else outside the marriage); Family; Friends; Work; Hobbies/Interests; Health/Fitness; Spirituality (whatever that means to the individual) and Self-improvement (whatever the individual is doing to improve themselves such as taking classes or self-help books or counseling, etc.). These components are illustrated below in what I refer to as The Goal Wheel:

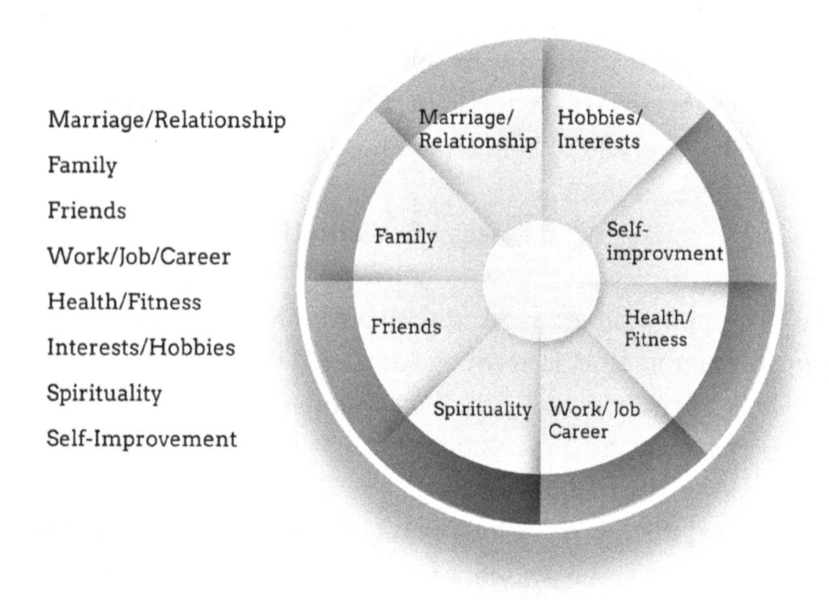

As you can see, there are eight components, and each one is in its own "pie slice." Each individual should seek to include each of these components in their life, and each has its importance. So, you may ask, shouldn't work occupy the most amount of area in The Goal Wheel since work occupies the most amount of time per day and week? Regarding "work," I contend that our job, work, or career shouldn't be the be-all, end-all, nor should it define our identity. However, we tend to identify ourselves by our work title. But, the wise individual, when asked who they are, they will ask, "In what context are you asking? My identity is incorporated in each of these eight components."

And, when it comes to work, I suggest that folks regarding The Goal Wheel put heavy boundaries around work so that work doesn't "bleed" into the other components. For example, when I counsel couples, and one of the spouses arrives home, they are still focused on work. I love to say to them, "You're cheating on your spouse. No, not physically, but you are not really with them. You have only physically changed zip codes from your work address to your home address. Yet, you are still thinking about, maybe consumed about, work." To these folks, I offer the following mental image. Imagine our minds are like computer chips; in this case, our mind has only two memory chips: our work and personal life. When you arrive at work, imagine yourself removing the memory chip that contains your personal life and replacing that memory chip with your work life. You will recall all the tasks that need your attention on that chip. Then, within the last hour of your workday, complete all tasks you can which take priority before leaving work. You want to say to yourself that whatever you didn't complete today will be there to finish tomorrow. Then, use your drive time home to transition from work to home. What do I want to do this evening or over the weekend that will occupy my time, attention, and thoughts and prevent me from thinking about work? Those endeavors could include spending quality time with your significant other, family, friends, etc. So, when you are back at work, you want to say to yourself, you know, when I was away from work, I didn't think about work, not even one nanosecond.

So, back to The Goal Wheel. Again, each component represents a "pie slice," and you can set short and long-term goals with each one. You may have to move one component from the back burner to the front burner, to set and accomplish a goal from a particular component or pie slice.

What makes life worth living are the goals we set and accomplish. Imagine each of us is in a rowboat. We decide on our destination (our goal) and how we will get there (our route). If we don't give up and "keep rowing," we will arrive at our destination. Avoid words like "try." Instead, commit to your efforts and implement action to achieve your goals. Once you have arrived (accomplished the plan/goal), relish in that accomplishment by rewarding yourself. Then, plot your next destination. The following quote is from Muhammad Ali, "He who is not courageous enough to take risks will accomplish nothing in life." This quote encapsulates my philosophy, utilizing my tenacity and never giving up, never waving a white flag in both attitude and spirit to accomplish short and long-term goals in my Goal Wheel.

As we get older, we often become more comfortable with ourselves and within our own skin. And along with age usually comes wisdom. I sometimes use the following with clients: "If you could go back in time and redo a period in your life, would you want to do so? But be careful. If you went back in time and could not take your wisdom, you might be bound to make the same mistakes the second time around." So, as we have gotten older, we have become more comfortable with ourselves. First, however, it is important to know thyself, including your strengths, what you have learned about yourself, what you learned from past experiences, what motivates you, and what goals you want to achieve, both short-term and long-term.

On the contrary, when individuals don't have goals to attain, they become stagnant and ripe for depressive symptoms because they have little to look forward to. Therefore, I often use The Goal Wheel to motivate and inspire my clients to be their best, which usually leads to a discussion on the term "self-actualization." In part, self-actualization is the realization or fulfillment of one's talents and potentialities, especially a drive or need in everyone. In addition, self-actualization is about achieving your dreams within your capabilities that spark your passion. One can ask their client to decide who they want to be. The only way to achieve self-actualization is to envision what their actualized self will look like. Connecting with one's future self is essential in reaching personal goals. Again, it is not just about helping clients be their best with their career goals but with every aspect of their lives.

Speaking of going back in time, one should be careful not to obsess about their past and perseverate on regrets. There isn't anything we can do about our history and those regrets; it should be in our rear-view mirror. The only thing the past is suitable for is to provide us with the wisdom of what we would do differently if a similar situation were to occur in the future. It is possible to have pleasant childhood memories and acknowledge the significant influencers in our lives. Still, the unpleasant ones often keep an individual stuck like a needle in a phonographic record.

10-5 Another Challenging Client

I would like to share one more client with you that exemplifies a counseling challenge for me but also is an example of how to use many techniques to assist that client. I have only seen this male client for less than ten sessions. The following is information about the client. When I began to see him, he was 26 years old; he is an only child of parents who had him when they were in their 40s. He had had some developmental issues and graduated from high school at a school that specialized in working with students with special needs. In his mid-20s, he is drastically overweight, with no hair on top of his head. His only hair was around the sides and the back of his head. He has never been gainfully employed. In the past, he took a few college classes at a community college but did not continue toward an associate's degree. He said he spends 8-10 hours playing video games, watching TV, and taking a nap each day, but to his credit, he admitted to walking on the treadmill for 15 minutes daily. Also, to his credit, he told his parents he would like to see a counselor again.

So, at his initial appointment, I inquired what happened and why he had seen therapists in the past, but that, over a short period, he did not continue. He said the last counselor would ask him at the beginning of each session what was new, and his reply was the same: "Nothing was new." He was following the same routine every day. None of the past clinicians had ever considered helping the client set any short- and long-term goals. He acknowledged that he knew his parents would not live forever and that he would need to work but didn't know how to achieve that realization. However, the client and his father shared that he loves computers and his ability to repair and build them from scratch.

His love for anything and everything related to computers led to a discussion about his enrollment in a class on cloud computing at a community college. Further counseling sessions were conducted to keep the suggestions very narrow in scope. For each appointment, only one recommendation was discussed on how he could successfully pass his class.

Other suggestions were offered at each session, and the client complied with every recommendation. He agreed to increase his time on the treadmill to 1 minute each week, slowly reduce the time spent playing video games, and gradually decrease the amount of food he consumes at each meal. This client was heavily praised for all of his efforts and progress toward each goal. I shared with him my beliefs that what makes life worth living is setting and accomplishing goals. Each morning, he could wake up thinking about how to make the most of every day. I informed him that clients come to counseling because there are things in their lives that they want to change, and I help them to achieve those changes by taking tiny incremental steps toward the eventual goals they want to achieve. As I do with every client, I continue to ask him periodically if I am meeting his needs and if the suggestions I offer are not overwhelming. As therapy continues, it appears that a successful rapport has been achieved.

Multitasking

When I was employed at the Federal EAP and was conducting presentations, we often discussed whether we could multitask. In my opinion, the answer is yes and no. Now that I have confused you, let me explain by offering examples. Let's say you are typing on your computer at work, and your work requires sustained attention. Then, the phone rings, and you decide to take the call. At the same time, the person on the other end of the phone wants to talk with you about something entirely different from what you are typing. So, the question is, can you give both tasks anywhere near 100% of your concentration? The answer you should conclude is that it is not possible to provide sustained attention to both tasks simultaneously.

So, is it possible to multitask at all? The answer is yes, but only when you have repeatedly done one of the tasks. One example would be when you were learning to tie your shoelaces as a child. Doing that, you could not think about any other task. Then, after you have mastered this task, you could tie your laces and think about other things simultaneously. Another example is when you learned how to drive a motor vehicle; it requires all or most of your attention. Now, as an adult, you are to drive and think about other things. Sometimes, we are so engrossed in our thoughts as though our vehicle was on auto-pilot, and we can't recall how we made it from point A to point B.

Procrastination

When it comes to courage and fears, I heard this quote and am unsure who should receive credit for it: "Courage is not the absence of fear; it's the overcoming of fear." So, overcoming procrastination can be applied with the following. Many folks, including clinicians, can experience and even struggle with procrastination. Some believe procrastination is not a laziness or time management problem, and I certainly agree with that belief. And some think it is a fear of success and a fear of failing.

Along with these fears, an individual may be consumed with negative self-talk and negative self-belief of themselves. So, the first step is to admit that one is procrastinating. The next step is to ask if these assertions are factual. The remedies include acknowledging irrational fears and combating those negative self-statements and beliefs by encouraging positive ones.

However, procrastination is not always about fears, negative self-belief, or self-talk. Instead, it can be the avoidance of something perceived as unpleasant and/or time-consuming. The tendency to procrastinate is something that I can relate to and has always been a challenge. For example, when employed with the Federal EAP, I immensely enjoyed conducting intakes and counseling new clients. However, when I completed that first session, I then had to input all that data into the EAP's computer. Even after having been with this EAP for many years, it would still take an hour to enter all the info into their system. Again, this process was both unpleasant and time-consuming. So, one of my solutions was to use the negative to motivate me to accomplish the task. I would typically start an intake at 9 am and finish with the client around 10:30. Then, I would ask if I wanted to eat lunch at noon. Of course, my answer was yes. So, I would tell myself that you can't have lunch until you enter the information into the computer. Another reason to avoid procrastinating in my example was that I disliked being behind in completing tasks. Therefore, each time

I began a project, I wanted to finish it to be even by the end of each day. I found it stressful to get too behind in completing those daily tasks. So, if I could not meet all the responsibilities at the end of a day, I would intentionally carve out as much time as needed the next day to complete the ones from the previous day before starting new ones.

Another way I found helpful in combating procrastination was establishing a task list that would help me stay organized and give structure to my day. I still make a task list every day, even in retirement. I even established a task list I wanted to complete each day while writing this book. So, the bottom line is to use one's tendency to procrastinate and instead motivate themselves by attaching a reward. Then, of course, they would implement that reward only after completing the task they were avoiding.

Stress Management

Whether it was conducting the presentation on Stress Management, when I was employed at the Federal EAP or helping clients struggling with stress, I enjoy helping folks to be able to manage their stress more effectively.

Again, I would use the illustration of Events/People and how one's Self -Talk leads to either Positive or Negative Emotions. I would offer the following example: Let's say that an individual has been laid off from their job, and in one scenario, their self-talk is negative (how am I/we going to pay my bills, we may have to sell our home, etc.). Their resulting emotions would be depression, anxiety, guilt, etc. I then ask my audience or clients if it is a foregone conclusion that one has to see being laid off from their job as a negative event. I offer that an individual could say (self-talk) how stressful the job was, and they will ensure their next job is less stressful. Therefore, their resulting emotions (from changing their negative self-talk to positive) could be confidence, empowerment, etc.

I also point out that two individuals could be compared to one another. For example, when encountering a stressor, one individual automatically reacts negatively while another person experiencing the same stressor responds differently. These people see themselves as being in charge of dealing with adversity. They say, "When others are losing their head, I will keep mine and will stay grounded." They will remind themselves of how they have successfully dealt with stress in the past, and then like a template, they can use their strategies to get through current and future stressors.

Did you know that all stress is negative and that there is a term for "good stress," and that word is "eustress?" First, of course, one needs to differentiate between stress (and perhaps eustress) and distress and how distress can impact our bodies, thoughts, feelings, and behaviors. Then, I emphasize to individuals how important it is to know thyself and take inventory of their strengths, attributes, and what they have learned from their past experiences. It is not in their best interest to dwell on their mistakes or regrets but only on what they have learned and what they will do if they are in a similar situation in the future. Finally, other stress management techniques are encouraged, such as deep breathing exercises, progressive muscle relaxation, listening to music, exercising, using humor, relying on one's support system, and avoiding coulda-shoulda-wouldas and instead, saying positive things to oneself that are inspiring and empowering. I like this quote from Irving Berlin, "Life is 10 percent what you make it and 90 percent how you take it."

Time Management

Time can be considered a commodity, a resource, but it differs from the others. Once one runs out of time, whether in a day or a week, one cannot be given any more.

If you multiply 24 hours a day times seven days a week, you know that there are 168 hours in a week. So, let us first address sleep. We are at our best when we obtain the required hours of sleep, not how many hours we can function but how much we need to feel rested when it is time to get out of bed. For most of us, that is between 6-8 hours. If we were to use the 8 hours of sleep a night as the figure, then that equals 56 hours of sleep for the week, subtracted from 168, which leaves 112 hours left for the week. If you work full-time, how many hours is that a week, let's say 40 hours? For clients who work longer than 40 hours a week, is the eventual goal is to get to 40 hours each week? If 40 hours a week is the number, that leaves 72 hours left for the week.

So, whether it is 40 40-hour work week or the 72 hours left over, the goal is to learn how to manage our time, behaviors, and tasks. The secret to managing these things is developing strategies to meet the time management challenge. Some of the suggestions I have mentioned in previous sections, such as having a checklist of tasks that need to be completed every day, not taking work home (either physically or mentally), establishing balance in one's life with engagement in interests, hobbies, having and spending time with friends, quality time with family and the accomplishment of goals in every facet of one's life. Additional keys to success are learning to be self-disciplined, being a self-starter, and setting boundaries.

Approach the concept of time as though you are in control of time (even though we can't). What does that mean? Some examples would include starting projects early so that you can complete them on or before deadlines. Also, good organizational skills can help with time management. Conversely, without mastering these skills, it is easier to flitter away valuable time we cannot retrieve.

I would like to introduce and share one last client with you. I first met him as a high school sophomore when he accompanied his mom after his father's death. He again requested counseling as a sophomore in college, said he wanted to work on some personal issues, and he said I was instrumental in his decision to become a therapist eventually. I decided to provide counseling to him in a different way, and I shared that with him. I proposed that while he was working on attaining his personal counseling goals, he could use some of the same strategies in helping his future clients. I also suggested that through therapy and as he is acquiring skills, he lists on paper his strengths, attributes, and strategies that aid him in establishing and maintaining his feeling of competence and confidence. I want to encourage you, the reader, to consider taking on this assignment. At the same time, you could also list lessons learned and avoid future pitfalls for yourself and advice you could offer to a colleague or a new clinician. The goal of this assignment is to strive to be the best therapist you can be.

An Acknowledgement To Those Who Inspired/Mentored Me

It is easy for me to accomplish this in print. However, for many, I wish I had let them know how they influenced me while they were still alive and that I had remained in contact with them. Of course, my first acknowledgment would have been to the psychologist who allowed me to meet with him when I was about the age of 13. I was able to conduct "informational interviews" with him twice a year until I graduated from high school. Nothing he ever said discouraged me; it only inspired me to pursue my career in psychology. Then, there were numerous professors and instructors who gave their time when I was both in undergraduate and graduate school. Again, I regret I hadn't stayed in contact with them to let them know how influential they were in helping me achieve my career goals.

Only recently did I successfully contact Dr. Stephen Davis, a former professor and advisor for my Master's degree thesis. I took every graduate course he taught while he was a professor at Austin Peay State University. I can still recall what I learned in his classes all those years ago. When I shared with him my desire to write this book, he offered to mentor me in the success of this undertaking. I cannot thank him enough. I also want to thank my friends and former colleagues, John

Thurman, Jack Jaffe, and Holly Germin, for their encouragement, invaluable feedback, and recommendations.

Another purpose in writing this section is to encourage the reader to reach out to those who inspired and mentored you. So, please remain in contact with them and tell them how much they meant to you.

I want to share another visualization with you. Imagine you and other clinicians are all mountain climbers, and each of you is at varying heights along that mountain. The more experienced ones are above you and lending a hand to you, assisting you to ascend to the same place they have achieved. This analogy can be applied to us as counselors. There are more experienced colleagues who are offering us the opportunity to benefit from their expertise. Then, as we gain more experience, we help those below us. The goal is to help each of us be the best clinician we can be. We accomplish this by writing and reading books on our profession, attending trainings, joining our professional organizations, and mentoring each other.

One of the items I wanted to accomplish in writing this book is encouraging and motivating the reader. Therefore, in Chapter 5, I shared some things I have accumulated and posted on bulletin boards in my office. I want to share some other motivational sayings. Here is one on life (author unknown): "Life is a challenge-meet it; Life is a gift-accept it; Life is an adventure-date it; Life is a sorrow-overcome it; Life is a tragedy-face it; Life is a duty-perform it; Life is a game-play it; Life is a mystery-unfold it; Life is a song-sing it; Life is an opportunity-take it; Life is a journey-complete it; Life is a promise-fulfill it; Life is beauty-praise it; Life is a struggle-fight it; Life is a goal-achieve it; Life is a puzzle-solve it." And here is one from Albert Einstein: "There are only two ways to live your life. One is as though nothing is a miracle. The other way is as though everything is a miracle."

And here is another quote on life by Harvey MacKay: "Life is too short to wake up with regrets. So, love the people who treat you right. Forget about the ones who don't. Believe everything happens for a reason. If you get a chance, take it, and if it changes your life, let it. Nobody said life would be easy, they just promised it would be worth it. Enjoy life now, it has an expiration date." Another picture I use with myself and my clients is to imagine our life as sand going through an hourglass. When we are young, we have a lot of time (sand), and it is easy to procrastinate or delay setting and achieving our goals. And before you know it, the sand is more than halfway through the hourglass.

For me, I knew when I was employed full-time and seeing clients in my part-time private practice that I did not have the time to write this book. When I retired from my full-time job at the age of 66, I was finally able to begin writing, and each day after breakfast, I sat in front of my computer. My logic was as follows: My father lived until he was 86, so if I remain in good health and live as long as he had, I could have 20 years left to accomplish the goals I have set. So, for each of us, the sand is continuing to run through the hourglass. Whatever goals (even if they appear to be out on the horizon) are important to you, set an arbitrary timetable to complete them and establish stepping stones or incremental smaller goals (baby steps) toward your overall achievement. And when you accomplish one, relish in that achievement and then set the next one. The accomplishment of your goals is what makes your life exciting and worth living.

I recently heard that former NASA astronaut Jose Hernandez was interviewed by Mike Huckabee on Huckabee's TV show. He said he had applied and was turned down at NASA 11 times before he was accepted into their program. He gave the 6-ingredient recipe to be successful in the career you choose. 1. Determine your purpose in life. 2. Recognize how far you need to travel to accomplish that goal. 3. Make yourself a roadmap. 4. Prepare yourself in accordance with the challenge. 5. Establish a work ethic second to none. 6. Perseverance.

And here is the last quote on life by Joyce Rawlings: "Life is not about waiting for the storms to pass... it is about learning how to dance in the rain. Be kinder than necessary because everyone you meet is fighting some battle." The last part of this quote reminds me of my former from my former professor, Dr. Edwin Timmons, who said, "We are all trying to get through this world the best way we know how."

So, I ended this book as I began. I am providing you with some new tools to put on your toolbelt and encourage you to continue to use the ones that may already be on your belt. The ones I have included in this book have helped me develop strategies and have benefited me in being successful with my clients. I hope my stories, techniques, and strategies will help you gain the confidence and competence to be the best therapist you can be in less time. I hope you will find your chosen career as rewarding as mine. I am borrowing a quote from author Marc Anthony, who wrote the following, "If you love what you do, you will never have to work a day in your life." I have offered this quote repeatedly to clients, colleagues, friends, and family, "If you have to get up every morning to go to a job, you might as well find a job/career that ignites your passion. Spending 30-40 years in a job or a profession you dislike will feel like a prison sentence." I am fortunate to have known the career field I wanted to pursue as an adolescent. In a span of over 40 years, I have only changed jobs (while remaining in the mental health field) four times. And I continue to offer my services in my private practice (counseling, health fairs, and CISMs). What a joyful ride it has been!

I have enjoyed writing this book with you, my readers, in mind, and again, I sincerely hope that it will be invaluable to you as you begin your career in helping others (from your clients to your colleagues). I welcome your feedback if you believe this book has benefited you. My email address is stevenmelman@yahoo.com. I shared my cell number in Chapter 9, but I will repeat it for those who didn't catch it: 214-728-0009. So, now, you have two ways to contact me.

References

Chapter 2

Thackeray Ritchie, Anne Isabella (First published in 1885). "Mrs. Dymond". Last edition was published on July 1, 1997, by Alan Sutton Publishing.

Miller, W. R., & Rollnick, S. (2013). *"Motivational interviewing: Helping people change"* (3rd edition). Guilford Press.

Duckworth, Sylvia. "The Iceberg Illusion".

Fagan, Abigail. (December 2022). "The 7 Traits of A Great Therapist." Psychology Today publication.

Chapter 3

Lieutenant Colonel West, Allen. "History is not there for you to like or dislike. It's there for you to learn from it. And if it offends you, even better. Because then you are less likely to repeat it. It is not yours to erase or destroy; it belongs to all of us." Fox News Interview. June 13, 2020.

President Ronald Reagan, at a press conference on August 12th, 1986, said, "The nine most terrifying words in the English language are I'm from the government, and I'm here to help."

President Ronald Reagan being interviewed by Mike Wallace of 60 Minutes in 1975.

Smith Gerald L. K, from his magazine, "The Cross and the Flag," in 1942.

The American School Counselors Association (ASCA) was held in Austin, Texas, in July of 2022, and the four-day seminar was entitled "No Limits."

https://www.verywellmind.com/ "what-is-inclusion"-5076061.

GW Online Public Health from November 5, 2020, entitled, "Equity vs. Equality, What's The Difference."

Comments by Carolyn Stone, the Ethics Chairman and past president of The American School Counselors Association (ASCA) conference. July 2022.

Roehikepartain, Jolene L "150 Ways To Show (Your) Kids You Care," Search Institute 2005.

Chapter 4

Devine, Miranda. "Did reefer drive the Highland Park parade 'killer... to madness?" The New York Post Opinion July 6, 2022.

Roberts, Dan. "Every Mass Shooting Shares One Thing In Common & It's Not Weapons." April 1, 2013. (https://www.ammoland.com/2013/04/every-mass-shooting-in-the-last-20-years-shares-psychotropic-drugs/#ixzz7Y1XLtbCQ

Shodair Children's Hospital and the article "Psychotropic Medications For Youth: Overview of Psychotropic Medications."

(https//mfpe.eventready.com/docs/download/Submission/Handouts/7961.pdf).

Monroe, Phillip. "Do Psychotropic Drugs Cause Violence and Aggression?" The Musings of a Christian Psychologist. June 20, 2015,

Iannarellli, John G. (2016) "How To Spot A Terrorist Before It Is Too Late," Safe Life Publishing, LLC.

The editor, not named, wrote "Marijuana Is The Common Web Between So Many Mass Killers July 3, 2018, from the publication "Parents Opposed To Pot: Bursting The Bubble of Marijuana Hype."

The National Institute of Health submitted the article "A Review of Cases of Pot And Violence" March, 2020.

Devine, Miranda "The Link Between Pot And Mass Shootings May Be Closer Than We Think." New York Post August 7, 2019.

Dr. Sharma, Pravesh. "How Teen Marijuana Use Impacts Brain Development." Mayo Clinic Health System. September 26, 2018.

Vyas, Hirva "Impact of Marijuana Use on Prevalence and Interventions in Peripheral Artery Disease",, Society for Cardiovascular Angiography & Interventions (SCAI) 2023 Scientific Sessions. May 18, 2023

"Crash Rates Jump in Wake of Marijuana Legalization New Studies Show." Insurance Institute For Highway Safety (IIHS). June 17, 2021.

Chapter 5

https://www.oxfordlearnersdictionaries.com/definition/english/xenophobia.

Cohut, Ph.D., Maria. "Global Impact of the COVID-19 Pandemic: 1 Year On." Medical News Today March 12, 2021.

Rogers, Kristen. Kristen Rogers, "Does Mask Wearing Harm Your Child's Development? Experts Weigh In" CNN Health August 21, 2021.

Mandel, Bethany. "Lockdowns Are Breaking Our Kids, And The Damage May Be Permanent," New York Post. July 17, 2022.

Camp, Patrick. "Report: Class of 2022 ACT Scores Lowest in Decades." The Cullman Times, Alabama. October 18, 2022, at 5:28 pm.

Sanchez, Ray. "' Nation's Report Card Shows New Evidence of COVID-19 Devastating Impact On US Children's Education," CNN. October 24, 2022.

Lee, Michael "Pandemic Learning Loss Could Cost Students Thousands In Income Over Their Lifetime: Study." Fox News December 29, 2022, 11:54 am EST.

Ament, Jill & Hart, Alexandra. "Study Finds COVID-Related School Closures Increased Mental Health Risks For Young People" from the publication Texas Standard: The National Daily News Show of Texas on July 21, 2022, 1:33 pm.

Chapter 6

Godek, Gregory J. P. "1001 Ways To Be Romantic" January 1, 1995.

"Fatherless Single Mother Home Statistics." 2013-2014. From the website "Fix Family Courts"

https://www.fixfamilycourts.com/single-mother-home-statistics/.

Chapter 7

"Sometimes You Have To Tell The Negative Committee That Meets Inside Your Head To Just Sit Down And Shut Up." Toby Mac Speak Life Quote on July 29, 2016.

Burns, David. "Feeling Good: The New Mood Therapy. Mass Market Paperback." January 1, 1980.

Miller, W. R., & Rollnick, S. *"Motivational interviewing: Helping people change"* (3rd edition). Guilford Press. 2013.

Chapter 8

Diller, Jerry V. "Cultural Diversity: A Primer For The Human Services", 4th Edition. Brooks/Cole Cengage Learning. 2011.

Alvoid, Tiffany. In a YouTube Ted Talk entitled, "Eliminating Microaggressions: The Next Level," December 9, 2019.

What is Critical Race Theory? Critical Race Training in Education. 2023.

Legg, Mark. "Is Critical Race Theory Marxist?" March 28, 2022. https://www.denisonforum.org/reources/is-critical-race-theory-marxist/.

Rantz, Jason. 'Math is Racist' Crowd Runs Rampant in Seattle, Portland." Newsweek. April 29, 2022 AT 6:00 AM EDT.

Dowling, M. "Study Examines Whiteness in Physics, Finds Whiteboards Are Racist." Independent Sentinel from March 22, 2022.

Dr. McDonald, Mark interview "The Dangers of Education." https://plandemicseries.com/education. 2023.

Coleman, Adam B. interview "Broken America: The Diversity Delusion." Jesse Kelly, The First TV. March 23, 2023.

Merriam-Webster Dictionary definition and meaning of Androgyny www.merriam-webster.com/dictionary/androgyny. August 26, 2021.

Dr. Grossman, Miriam testified before the House Committee On Energy and Commerce. YouTube. June 23, 2023.

Prestigiacomo, Amanda, "Jordan Peterson Talks Gender Ideology." Daily Wire January 26, 2022.

Wright, Ph.D., Colin. "Sex Is Binary." From Prager University, 2023.

Peterson, Jordan. Transgenderism interview by Ben Shapiro. YouTube: Ben Shapiro. December 18, 2018.

Clements, KC Clements. "Can Men Become Pregnant?" Healthline. December 20, 2018.

"Wisconsin Middle Schoolers Charged With Sexual Harassment For Failing To Use Preferred Pronouns." Legal Insurrection. (legalinsurrection.com). Saturday, May 14, 2022, at 09:05 pm.

Duggan, Laurel. "Yes, Doctors Are Performing Sex Change Surgeries on Kids." The Daily Caller. August 18, 2022.

Ennis, Dawn. "More US Hospitals Offering Gender-Affirming Surgeries." NBCNews.com. October 31, 2016.

Ennis, Dawn. "More U.S. Hospitals Offering Gender-Affirming Surgeries." NBCNews.com. October 31, 2016.

Rachmuth, Sloan Founder & President of Education First Alliance North Carolina

https://www.edfirstnc.org. Interviewed by Liz Wheeler from the Liz Wheeler Show. May 19, 2023.

Yandell, Kate. "Young Children Do Not Receive Medical Gender Transition Treatment." FactCheck.org. May 5, 2023.

Rachmuth, Sloan. "Duke Doctor Giving Puberty Blockers To Second Graders,"

https://www.edfirstnc.org. June 6, 2023.

Rachmuth, Sloan. "Panic Mode: Duke & UNC Deny ECU Wrongdoing In Treating Transgender Toddlers." https://www.edfirstnc.org. May 5, 2023

Rachmuth, Sloan. "ECU To Sue Education First Alliance For Reporting Its Gender Clinic," https://www.edfirstnc.org. May 10, 2023.

"Vanderbilt Hospital: Gender Reassignment a 'Money Maker,' Threatens Doctors Who Object." The Conservative Post. September 21, 2022.

Dreher, Rod. "Vanderbilt Hospital: Gender Reassignment a 'Money Maker,' Threatens Doctors Who Object." The Conservative Post. September 21, 2022.

Gender dysphoria–NHS (www.nhs.uk). May 28, 2020.

Trafalgar Poll October, 2022.

Ciancio, Susan. "How Many Trans People Regret Transitioning?" Human Life International. 2015.

Dutch News: "Gender doubts are a "normal part of growing up" study." Gender doubts are a "normal part of growing up": study–DutchNews.nl March 15, 2024.

Hopkins, Steve. "Influencer Who Transitioned Into A Korean Woman Is Now Transitioning Back Into A British Man." "JOE." An online publication. December 11, 2022.

"Magnum Force," Clint Eastwood's character Harry Callahan, famous quote: "A man has to know his limitations." 1973.

Chapter 10

Karnes, Barbara. "Gone From My Sight: The Dying Experience." Barbara Karnes Publishing. January 1, 2008.

Liles, Maryn. "Need Some Motivation? These 125 Inspiring Quotes From Boxing Legend Muhammad Ali Are Here to Help." Parade Magazine. May 19, 2023.

The Harvey Mackay Archives. The Thrive Time Show. https//www.harveymackay.com.

Hernandez, Jose, NASA Astronaut Interviewed by Mike Huckabee on his show Huckabee on TBN. September 23, 2023.

Living Legend Joyce Rawlings – Living Legends of Alexandria (alexandrialegends.org) April 15, 2015.

Printed in the USA
CPSIA information can be obtained
at www.ICGtesting.com
LVHW012331011024
792705LV00014B/625

9 781662 899461